I Loved a Boy

Confessions of a Roman Catholic Priest

By Reverend James L. Meyer

Van Antwerp and Beale Publishers

Van Antwerp and Beale Publishers

2222 Lloyd Avenue, Royal Oak, Michigan 48073-3849
(248) 541-1788 – E-Mail: gvanantwerp1@comcast.net
International Standard Book Number (10) 0-9759416-3-1
International Standard Book Number (13) 9780975941638
Printed in the United States
First Edition
Library of Congress Control Number: 2006940168

Cover by Rachel Timlin
www.thenewgenericbrand.com

Photo selection by Debbie Ajini
of,
"Designs by a Genie"

Reviews

Jim, I have been on retreat all day long with your writing. It is superb, especially the trip on the train. It is a very unique kind of writing and a whole unique area. This book will be of great consolation to countless people.

> *The late Father Edward J. Farrell, widely acclaimed author of books on spirituality, international retreat and spiritual director, member of the faculty (1961-1978) and spiritual director (1967-1978) at Sacred Heart Seminary in Detroit, Michigan.*

Jim, I stand in amazement and awe at your courage. I finished your book, "Confessions of a Roman Catholic Priest". It is great. It speaks of a warmly human and caring man who is not afraid of true intimacy. I bet there will be a fallout for you, but I think your book should be a "must read" for seminarians who will commit to living a life of celibacy. Well done.

> *Thomas Gumbleton, auxiliary bishop of Detroit*

About the Author

Rev. James L. Meyer, MA, JD

James L. Meyer has undergraduate degrees from Sacred
Heart Seminary College in Detroit and Catholic University
of America, in Washington, D.C. He has a Master's in
International Relations from Georgetown University
Graduate School of Foreign Service and Government and a
Juris Doctor from Detroit College of Law. On a recent
sabbatical, he took women's studies courses at the
University of Detroit Mercy.

Rev. Meyer directed the Pastoral Care Department of
Hutzel Hospital in the Detroit Medical Center for over a
third of a century where his chosen specialties were
gynecologic oncology, orthopedics, intensive care and
biomedical ethics. At various times, staff and/or volunteer
chaplain at Children's Hospital of Michigan and Harper
Hospitals, he specialized in cystic fibrosis and intensive
care.

Jimeyer has served on the boards of Michigan Pulmonary Disease Community, Inc. (MPDCI), Metropolitan Detroit Chapter of the Cystic Fibrosis Foundation, Contemporary Art Institute of Detroit (CAID), Kensington Academy, Chateau Chantal Winery and Inn in Traverse City, Michigan and Mendoza, Argentina, as well as the Professional Advisory Committee of Karmanos Hospice Program and the Biomedical Ethics Committee of the Wayne County Medical Society (WCMS).

Fr. Meyer continues as an active Roman Catholic priest with the Archdiocese of Detroit with 47 years of service. He is also an attorney and certified social worker, specializing in grief counseling, both licensed by the State of Michigan. Current activities include consulting chaplain for critically and terminally ill youth, management of Chalfonte House and Ryan Giannini Park (RGP) and directing the Chalfonte Foundation (www.chalfonte.org) as President and CEO.

Jim proudly resides in the city of Detroit.

Author's quote:
"Ryan had a way, on this occasion and several others, of extracting my heart, expanding its capacity a hundredfold while insinuating himself inside, and then gently replacing it back into my body."

About the book:
Many times in our lives, all of us have had loves, and all of us have had losses. "I Loved a Boy" is a paradigm for both love and loss from the perspective of a unique, unorthodox, countercultural application of professional and personal norms and relationships between two individuals separated in age by generations.

Though the book will resonate with the experiences of every person, it is meant neither for children nor the squeamish of heart or faith. It distills the author's lifetime of reflection on love, pain and loss, epitomized in the unanticipated death of a loved one to whom he had become extravagantly close. The writing reflects the educational as well as the experiential background of the author, but is neither ponderous nor philosophical. One will find herein both humor and cleverness, notably in the antics of the often terminally ill children vacationing at Chalfonte House.

In roughly a third of the book, referred to in chapters headed "Journal of Grieving", the author not only bares his soul, but carefully delineates feelings versus reason, and faith and trust versus blind submission to religious doctrine in the grieving process. If you look for reliance on traditional preaching or pious clichés to resolve issues of love and loss, you won't find them in this book. What you will find is a much broader spiritual journey that ultimately leads to comfort, consolation and closure.

Dedication

To Andrew Peter, Ryan, Matthew … and all the
kids who've taught me how to love.

Acknowledgements

First and foremost to the late *Fr. Edward J. Farrell*, spiritual director of Sacred Heart Seminary and author of twelve books on spirituality who had prodded me for years to write the stories of the kids. He was effusive in his praise of <u>this</u> work to within an hour of his death. *Judy Bobrow,* as admiring of my ministry as she was meticulous in her editing. *Robert Blair Kaiser,* who insisted the job of the author was not to write but to rewrite and that I should propel all my adverbs to Lourdes to hang up with the other crutches. *Carla Vollmer* an inspiration and companion on our mutual journey for over two decades and an author herself. *Maureen Feighan Kurth,* who refused to do it for me, insisting I could write. *Rich & Cindy Giannini,* Ryan's parents, whose constant mantra was "don't change a word." *Ryan, Maggie and Emily Upson* who would not tolerate even a grammatical article to be out of place. *Robert P. Begin* and *Rev. Robert Singelyn,* classmates and friends for almost sixty years, whose keen eyes caught the obvious, that had eluded me after many readings, *Paul M. Hresko,* whose pointed observations were invaluable for a final tidy copy.

I am a fairly good homilist, but hesitant writer; there were countless others whose encouragement and criticism helped hone these pages. Lastly to all the children and adults, named or anonymous to you but not to me, who have been an intimate part of my ministry and my life for over seventy years. Attribute to them any gold you might unearth from these pages. The dross is mine.

Foreward

What does a mom say when she's told a book would be written about her son who had unexpectedly passed on? Tears came to my eyes when Jimeyer told me he wanted to share Ryan's story. I was deeply touched by his gesture because I knew this would be done honestly with love expressed from deep within his heart.

Those who never knew Ryan would now learn about my hero, my suffering servant, my inspiration. They would read of the example he set to those who did know him because of his tremendous strength, acceptance of whatever obstacle came his way and, most impressive, his sense of humor through it all.

Even though he was a visitor on this earth for what some may consider a short time, I believe he accomplished everything he was sent here to do. He learned the important things in life which some never learn, even during their long lifetime.

I'm glad you will have the opportunity to meet Ryan and some of Jimeyer's other special kids throughout this book. One day I too would like to write my own on my belief in Ry's continual strong spiritual influence on me as his spirit lives on. Until that time, I can only say how grateful I am for Jimeyer's dedication to Chalfonte. I also feel truly blessed that I was chosen to be Ryan's mom… forever. ☺

TRUST – BELIEVE – SMILE

Cindy Giannini
Mother of Ryan   *May, 2005*

vii

Foreward

In the early summer of 1960 Fr. James L. Meyer was assigned to Sacred Heart Parish, Dearborn, in the Archdiocese of Detroit. It was his first assignment as a newly ordained priest. I was an altar boy of fourteen. Our meeting was the beginning of a friendship that has spanned forty-seven years.

In 1969, "Jimeyer", that's the elision of names first used by my children to address The Reverend James L. Meyer Esq., was engaged in a "disagreement" with the Archdiocese over questions of "due process" (fundamental fairness) within the Church, that led to his reassignment as chaplain of Hutzel and Children's Hospitals in Detroit. Early that year, I had been indicted for refusing induction into the Armed Services of the United States because of conscientious objection and was facing trial and a possible five year jail sentence.

We did what any reasonable young men would do in those days under those circumstances; we took a 4,000 mile road trip across the country. One of our two immutable rules was not to take the Interstate Highways. The first stop was a State campground in northern Michigan on the shores of Lake Michigan. It was early in the afternoon so we set up camp and went for a swim. People have told me that the waters of the Great Lakes in the north warm up. It's not true. As I walked in, Jimeyer ran past me, dove in, reappeared a few seconds later and let out an ear piercing yell:

YES!!!!!!!!!!!!.

Our second rule was not to put the top up on his Fiat convertible 124 Sports Spider. After all, we weren't afraid of getting wet.

I realized then that his life was being written in bold type and exclamation marks, mine in italics and parentheses.

Over the years we have shared counsel and comfort and become uncontrollably irritated with each other. We have laughed and cried together. He presided at my wedding, baptized my children, buried my father and mother, presided at the weddings of my married children and consoled me when my younger brother died. After Ryan died he asked me to create a reliquary for Ryan's ashes that his parents would put in a small meditation room converted from Ryan's bedroom.

We have learned much from each other.

Over the years I have come to believe that there is no such thing as "trickle down Christianity" any more than there is "accidental love" or a "war to end all wars". The simple precepts of behavior and core beliefs of Christianity must be acted out in the flesh. It is only then that the promise of peace can be fulfilled, internally generated and externally manifested. I have come to believe that the experience of true Christian spirituality is the liberation of love.

"I Loved a Boy -- Confessions of a Roman Catholic Priest" is a love story. It is a love story that stands in the face of, and challenges the paralyzing response to the revelations of clerical sexual abuse within the Roman Catholic Church. At its core it contradicts the sense of entitlement on the part of certain priests that led to the violation of innocents that robbed them of their first life-affirming experiences of freely chosen expressions of sexual love. This book challenges the assumption that distance and demeanor can mask that sense of entitlement. It is a love story, the telling of which has its risks, exposure of the author's vulnerability among the greatest risks.

I Loved a Boy

The "Confessions" referred to in the title, are not the confessions of sin and guilt that lead to need for forgiveness, but confessions as we see them in the work of St. Augustine. They are the expression of deeply held beliefs, feelings and the life generated by them. These confessions are the celebration of those gifts "a Deo datus", "given by God".

Is love a belief? Is it a state of being? Can it exist disembodied as Plato might have us believe? Perhaps. I'm neither a great believer in Platonic love nor Cartesian duality. And although I love St. Francis of Assisi and the impact of his teaching on world civilization, I would not be inclined to refer to my body, as "brother ass" as he did. I know when I have been an ass, in body, mind and spirit. There is no blaming my obstinacy, ignorance, or stupidity on a concept of the separation of body and soul. I can be, have been, and I'm sure, on occasion, will continue to be a holistic ass.

At the risk of new age cliché', when I consider the amount of energy; heart pumping, liver functioning, lungs oxygenating, cells dividing and synapses firing; it takes to generate even a reed-thin thought, I am convinced that spirituality/love is the result of a collaborative effort taking place within the confines of our bodies. How could I be transported to the point of ecstasy if my blood were not circulating? And, since spirituality/love is a collaborative effort, it has much to do with the functioning of the bodies around us.

Why am I saying this? This "Confession" stands in the face of deeply ingrained and accepted concepts of beauty prevalent in the western world, especially American. We have been taught to believe that physical attractiveness is a precursor to love, validation and acceptance. The classical Greeks taught us the concept of perfect form. I really don't believe any of it -- well, I don't believe 66% of it.

I have spent forty years as a sculptor. As such it has been my duty (it's a tough job...) to look at, model and appreciate beautiful, usually nude human beings. I have taught figure modeling. My work has bored and excited me. I have looked at tons of living human flesh which has led me to believe that there is no real measure of human beauty. I have had three favorite models.

The first was a woman who modeled for a life drawing class I was taking at the Center for Creative Studies, now College for Creative Studies, in Detroit. She was in her mid-seventies. Her skin was not stretched over her skeleton and musculature, it was draped. Every time she changed a pose it was like looking at a different person. Every surface shifted. She had a face full of mischief that belied her age. Her experience as a model made her a joy with whom to work.

The next was a man who modeled for me when I was teaching a sculpture class at Wayne State University in Detroit. The class was scheduled late so I took the only model available. Harry came into the studio with a book in hand, something by Kafka or Kant, something to read in case we decided on a seated pose. He was big, tall and doughy. His hair was tied back in a pony tail that went to the middle of his back. His glasses slid halfway down his large nose. Harry was hairy. I wasn't sure I could look at this guy for the next six weeks. But he was a wonderful model, mountainous in form, a Balzac without the robe, and he was experienced. He modeled for me on a regular basis after that semester.

The third was a model to whom Harry introduced me. He had gotten a job as a parking lot attendant and his work conflicted with my class schedule. He asked me if I would

mind if Celeste took his place. She didn't have a lot of
experience. Celeste was almost as tall as Harry, mid-
twenties, blond and a dancer. Her skin stretched over her
skeleton and musculature. I told Harry I wouldn't mind.
Like I said, the Greeks were about a third right.

Ryan had Gorham's Syndrome (Wasting Bone Disease).
The effects on his appearance were a source of anguish.
That anguish was a source of his rapier wit and expansive
humor. Jimeyer? I don't think he's going to make it to the
cover of *GQ* or *Esquire*. These two loved each other
because a long line of "coincidences" propelled them
together. They loved each other because they grew to love
each other. They loved each other because they chose to
love each other. Theirs was not a love that separated body,
mind and spirit. To paraphrase Michigan's State motto --"*If
you seek something beautiful; look around you* . And they
did.

The story of Chalfonte House unfolds in this book. It is a
story of a gestating community of young people, wise
beyond their years, who empower each other, not because
they are physically "compromised" but because that's what
people in love do. It is a story of the "temporarily able-
bodied" that is a frame for persons who love and respond to
them and those who are uncomfortable with them and close
down.

In this beautifully transparent narrative, an exposed and
vulnerable Roman Catholic priest, who has faced his
ministry and relationships fearlessly, challenges all of us to
do the same. Is it fear of judgment, is it fear of retribution,
chastisement or rejection, is it fear of death that paralyzes
us in the face of intimacy? How do we answer our fears?
What must we risk in order to live?

Molly Bloom, James Joyce's sensuous female character in

Ulysses, speaks a poignant expression of acceptance and surrender in the final lines of the book. The main character, Leopold Bloom, not unpurposefully, wanders the streets of Dublin. He knows that his wife, Molly, an opera singer, is going to meet with her agent, Blazes Boylin, to arrange a performance. Boylin has more in mind. Bloom knows he can't prevent it. Bloom hasn't consummated his relationship with Molly since his new born son, Rudy, died shortly after birth eleven years ago. Leopold is not terrified of love, but of the physical expression of it and the consequences of that expression. His only son died. Who could risk another loss? Love is dangerous.

Molly, in desperation, commits adultery with Boylin, a man she doesn't love. As the man she loves sleeps with his head at the foot of the bed, impotent with fear, she fantasizes about their first sexual encounter -- the day he proposed -- and says:

"...YES his heart was going like mad and YES I said YES I will. YES."

I mentioned earlier that Jimeyer had commissioned me to create a reliquary for Ryan's ashes. I believe it is testimony to Ryan's devious wit that I either miscalculated the volume or got the wrong information. The reliquary was too small. Ryan's remains -- the ones that could not be contained -- were scattered in Grand Traverse Bay, part of the great fresh water sea that surrounds us.

He was not afraid of the water.   YES!

Love is a state of being.   Yes.

Hugh Timlin
February, 2007

Introduction

This book is about my love for a boy that is warm, intimate and passionate. It is about my relationships with kids, alone or together, who have played in my yard, supped at my table and slept in beds adjacent to my own. They often have been looked upon as damaged goods - not worth the attention of their fast-paced peers. I have enfolded them in my arms, their tears mingling with my own, as we cared for each other.

On top of my cluttered bedroom dresser, I have a singular graduation photo of Ryan Giannini, the boy I had known and loved since we first sat together on his bed at Children's Hospital of Michigan to watch the summer storms. He was fourteen then, and we discovered our mutual awe of lightning, thunder and torrential rains. The more intense the storms, the better. We ranked them on an arbitrary scale of one to five.

At age eighteen he wrote on the photo:

> To Jimeyer – If anyone deserves a picture of me it's definetly (sic) you. For all that we've been through together, I think you deserve it. You have been a great friend, teacher and mentor to me. These past few years have been absolutly (sic) awesome, and I look forward to many more. Thank you! Love, Ryan.

And this from a teenage boy to an unrelated "Father" distanced in years by half a century.

I was ill prepared for his final days on earth at age twenty.

I Loved a Boy

Tim Burgess had moved out west, but had returned with other "Chalfonte Kids" for what turned out to be the week before Ryan's death. For years the two had communicated in person and through the Internet. Their relationship had been forged in the kiln of mutual childhood suffering. As a teen, Tim had had an amputation secondary to bone cancer. At age twenty, he had the distinction of being the only one-legged bicycle messenger in Denver, Colorado. From the anguish of their geographic separation, Tim charged me to read the following e-mail at the bedside of a comatose Ryan in Detroit.

> Ryan, when I first heard that you were in the hospital my first instinct was to try to figure out how I could possibly get to you to show you how much I care, and just generally be there for you. Maybe it is just an unspoken bond between us that you know how much I truly care about you and how big a part of my life you are, but it can't hurt to tell you. I cherish every conversation we have whether it be spiritual, political, perverted, or just about nothing at all. You are a best friend in every sense of the word, and I love you for it. Tim.

Ryan's death has made me raise my palms heavenward to cry irrationally: "Damn the hospitals --- that could not move timely air into the lungs of my beloved! Damn the phantoms sneering at me beneath the mask of 'uncertain world- renowned procedures' that contributed to blocking his airway. "

The Scripture resonates with my despair:

"A voice is heard in Ramah, lamentation and bitter

weeping. Rachel is weeping for her children: she refuses to be comforted for her children, because they are no more". (Jeremiah 31:15)

I am aware that by confessing my love for a boy, I am exposing my guarded self to scrutiny and speculation. Even as I pen these words, I see a thousand eyebrows raised in horror and disbelief. Although I do not welcome exposing my personal feelings in print, I must tell the story of my relationship with a boy to counteract sinister forces in the world that work against everything I believe.

First of all, I want to contradict the prevailing ethos that leaves unchallenged the belief that life without coitus is life without sex or passion. Amidst the pale that shrouds Catholic priests, there are many of us who live lives overflowing with both love and intimacy from sundry sources. My career has been the antithesis of sterility and impotence. Oh God, deliver us from human encounters that lack passion! The boys and their families could testify whether our relationships were perverse or mutually wholesome, healing and life-giving.

Secondly, I want to counteract the cloud of faceless anonymity, fear, misunderstanding and anxiety surrounding us that makes us suspicious of everyone different from ourselves. This kind of thinking leads us to a national frenzy of name-calling, war-talk, violence and destruction as ways to solve our differences. It is the thinking that makes it impossible for us to see the human face of those we call our enemy. It leads to torture and perversions of the grossest kind, perpetrated by those who otherwise would be seen as decent and moral human beings.

I ask myself – "How is it possible for my encounters with Ryan and other boys and girls I have known to have awakened in me, an old man who all his life has been insulated from sexual intimacy by the mandate of his Church, such a profound awareness of virility, fatherhood and humanness?"

As I have dared to expose my heart and soul, and the hearts and souls of these special kids, I challenge you to open yours to the stories, songs, humor and hidden secrets revealed in these pages. I hope you will see through these stories that we are sustained in life, not by potions and prescriptions or other allopathic interventions, however pertinent they may be, but by the unconditional love of family and friends. And that love includes intimacy that ought not to be thwarted by personal or national fear or an all-inclusive imposition of rules and regulations.

Pain and pathos are interwoven with counsel, comfort and comedy; much from the lips of the children themselves. Many stories emerge from experiences at Chalfonte House, my vacation cottage described in chapter one. Herein is significance for all of us. The lives of these children and their relationships provide inspiration needed to muddle through the maze of our own confused lives, to seek a true alignment of values and authentic peace within our nation, our world and ourselves.

CONTENTS

The Tree of Life
at Chalfonte House

Chapter 1: The Beginning

Call me, "Jimeyer".

"Jimeyer" ---one word.

"Jimeyer," begins the voice on my phone. It is my friend and colleague, Mary Piercey Kraft. My relationship with Mary, her late husband Greg, and her three boys - Aric, Ben and *Jon, (also known as *Piecey for a very funny reason) goes back to the time when the boys, now all in their 20s, were preadolescents and "Chalfonte Kids."

Chalfonte House is the 125-year-old renovated Victorian home in Elk Rapids, Michigan, to which my parents retired in 1977 before they both died in the mid-1980s. There are five bedrooms, a "lodge room", solarium-den, three living rooms, three baths, three kitchens and a basement recreation space called "The Trophy Room." Gracing one corner of the Trophy Room is a large mural of a spreading tree. Each kid signs a leaf with the date she or he first came to Chalfonte. Parents sign the trunk. A second mural covers the ceiling with clouds, comets and constellations. Thereon is inscribed the name of each Chalfonte kid who has died -- more than fifty at the time of this writing. All these kids are trophies, *more precious than gold.* My semi-private quarters are referred to as the "geriatric" area. Chalfonte House is owned by General Motors Acceptance Corporation (GMAC) and me. GMAC owns most if it.

A veteran "Chalfonte Kid" is a person of whatever age, who has fulfilled the following non- negotiable conditions:

Jimeyer with two other bald-headed guys
(Craig Richards and Eddie Carter)
at the entrance of Chalfonte House

1. As a rookie, located the house. We don't give "directions," though sometimes we allocate a key to be tried in the locks of the doors of the house the rookie believes to be the destination.
2. Stayed overnight.
3. Made a foray to the local compactor with the week's trash and recyclables. I tout this as "the highlight of their stay."
4. Written of their activities in the Chalfonte House Guest Book, of which to date there are eight volumes.

I recall Craig Richards, who died of osteosarcoma (bone cancer) at age seventeen on November 8, 1998. Craig was so quiet it was difficult for me to assess whether he had had a good time at Chalfonte. "You know Craig," I challenged, "you do not get invited back unless you write in the guest book about your week's adventures!" His entry was true to his character. "Jim: Fun – Craig."

"Jimeyer," Mary calls on the phone on an evening in July of 1996. I had introduced myself to Mary years ago when I celebrated weekend Mass at St. Dennis Parish in Royal Oak, Michigan. The joy of her music and her voice mesmerized me as she played guitar and sang for the services. I have commissioned her to play for many of the funerals of the kids.

For more than thirty-six years my assignment by the Archdiocese has been as chaplain to critically and terminally ill children. It was not a job I had chosen. This was to be a temporary assignment to Children's and Hutzel hospitals in the Detroit Medical Center until another parish assignment could be determined for me. I never wavered from my choice at age eight to become the pastor of a parish. That is the vocation for which I had been accepted after twelve years of seminary training. That is the career pathway I had embraced at ordination in 1960 and I wanted to continue on it without these hospital detours.

Through a colleague, Sr. Joyce Deshano, SSJ, I learned the poignancy of ministry to the sick and dying, trebly precious when children were involved. I muse at how unanticipated vistas beckon and we often first respond with heels dug deep in resistance.

"Jimeyer," Mary said, as she called from her position as child life specialist at Henry Ford Hospital, on West Grand Boulevard in Detroit. "Do you take consultations?" Knowing my answer before I could respond she tantalized, "I have a fourteen-year-old who is being transferred to the intensive care unit (ICU) at Children's Hospital. He's your kind of kid."

Thus begins my intimate relationship with a boy I came to love. The story she unfolded was this.

Ryan Giannini had spent seven weeks at Ford Hospital. Not only was he bored, but he needed money for a new printer for his computer. He cajoled his mother into stopping at the Meijer's store on her way to the hospital to pick up candy, pop, snacks and other items. He opened "Ryan's Store," advertising by word of mouth, overhead announcements and special handout bulletins.

"Ryan's stuff is cheaper and better than what you can find in the cafeteria," he touted, "and there are specials with every dollar's purchase." Nurses and other hospital personnel flocked to his room. The handwritten ledger listing every transaction, with special attention to profit margins, remains among Ryan's personal effects.

The following account of the operation may be apocryphal,

4

but this is the way I remember Ry telling it to me in that summer of 1996.

Some Ford Hospital officials had no sense of humor or appreciation for the entrepreneurial spirit of a fourteen-year-old patient. Threat of a shutdown loomed large. So he negotiated fifteen percent for charity --- and Ryan's Store was up and humming.

That was not Ry's only joust with authorities at Ford Hospital during this stay. His companion was Tetris, a guinea pig named after the Super Nintendo game he loved to play. His mom had sought and been granted permission from the nursing manager of the pediatric unit for the animal to be with Ry. After all, he had a private room and had been caring for guinea pigs since age four. Further, the Michigan Humane Society had assured his mom that the only problem might be if someone allergic to dander would pick him up --- the pig --- not Ryan.

It turned out that dangerous dander was not the pig's sole problem. In pranced Dr. Whosit (not his real name) from infectious disease. Protestations from mom concerning how the pet was comforting to Ryan and how it helped in his recovery were met with, "That pig has to go"!

Ryan was not cowered either by the doctor's edict or his arrogance. "He's not going home till I go home," he retorted. "We'll see," was the doctor's parting volley. "The doctor was not happy at all and said he'd be back after he talked to whomever. I don't remember because I was ticked," Ry's mom recalls. "I prepared a speech I intended to use stating my case against the higher-ups when they would come back and tell us no. To our surprise, the doctor came back later that day and said he could stay." --- the pig --- and Ryan.

5

The staff loved having Tetris around. When they came into Ryan's room they would share stories of the pets they had. As with all his animals, Ryan took good care of Tetris, brushing him daily and cleaning his cage. But Tetris only lived about three years and after his death, Ryan did not want another guinea pig.

"Indeed, my kind of kid!" I mused, reflecting on the Ryan's Store operation. Since second grade, I have been renowned for my prowess in multiplying a dollar -- whatever the cause. I was to learn that Ryan and I had another virtue in common. Both of us were cheap. Cheap is below frugal --- and both of us wear that appellation as a badge of honor.

I donned my business suit --- shirt, tie, the whole bit. Without close scrutiny, one of my backgammon sets looks similar to a briefcase. I walked to Children's Hospital of Michigan to meet my referral. "Mr. Ryan Giannini?" I challenged as I entered the cubicle in ICU where a diminutive adolescent was bedded. Ignoring his blank and startled stare as well as a figure in the shadows I presumed to be his mother, I continued. "My name is James L. Meyer and I'm an attorney (true) --- AND I WANT TO BE YOUR AGENT!"

Over several weeks of his hospitalization, Ry and I had many visits, frequently with his mother present; often just the two of us in his private room. The bond cemented when we realized that both of us were fascinated by summer lightning storms. It helped that his room faced south. We sat together on his bed and watched the displays in silence, waiting until the end to rank them on our arbitrary scale of one to five. I taught him backgammon, which he came to love to play ---- for money!
"This young man, now known to all of us well, was seen

today (August 19, 1996) for a postoperative visit," reports Arvin I. Phillippart, M.D., pediatric thoracic surgeon at Children's Hospital, to another of Ryan's many doctors, Henry Bone III, M.D., (yes, that is his real name) endocrinologist at Henry Ford Hospital.

> As you will recall, he had a prolonged hospitalization for extensive pleural fluid accumulation coincident to his Gorham's syndrome. Prolonged thoracostomy tube drainage of as much as 600-700 ml per day ultimately became ineffective with accumulation of a large intrapleural coagulated fluid collection. Because of major problems in anesthetic management of his upper airway associated with his maxillary and mandibular disease, he was transferred (here) to Children's for thoracotomy with evacuation of a very large amount of coagulated lymph within his pleural space as well as pleurodesis. At the time of operation he was noted to have complete right lung atelectasis with 2000-2500 cc of coagulated fluid. He was also noted to have extensive involvement of characteristic lymph hemangiomatosis of his chest wall prior to entering his pleural space....

The rest of the post-operative report of a successful surgical intervention need not be quoted. Suffice it to say, Ry was not a healthy puppy. My bias, honed over thirty years of working with sick and dying children, is that how well they cope with illness, indeed how long they live, is proportionate to how they are treated as "normal" within the structure of their family and society.

I noted how well Ryan was integrated in his family. Over the years I have known him, I have used the Gianninis as a model of how to treat a child with special needs. Ryan's parents, Cindy and Rich, treated him as their middle child.

He received no quarter for being sick ---- nor did he seek it.
He idolized his older brother Chad --- and spent less time
than in earlier years with his younger sister Jill, when as a
teen she began to have other boys in her life. Typical.

Cindy would defer to his physical limitations. She was
there for him when multiple attacks of his disease left him
vulnerable, experimented upon and hospitalized.

Both Ryan and I are middle children. I believe the clichés
attributed to such. We are fierce and independent survivors.
"And how about your classmates?" I inquired of him,
knowing that he was home schooled during junior high
years. "They don't come around much any more," was his
wistful response. I vowed to change that.

It was the rare occasion when Ry would share his deepest
concerns. He guarded his privacy. With the precision of the
accountant he aspired to be, he parsed out to different
persons various concerns of his life and growing up. Mostly
he kept them to himself. The last thing he would tolerate
was sympathy.

His compromised oral anatomy distorted his appearance
and made his speech difficult to understand. Looks mean
little to me. I was never a handsome guy. As the
relationship between Ryan and me grew more intimate, his
disfigurement faded into nothingness. And I got good at
interpreting his patois.

After his death, with prompting from his mother, I am able
to construct an accurate medical history. From this, one can
understand the reasons for the malformations of his face
and body.

When Ryan was seven the following symptoms began to

emerge. His lower teeth started to loosen and his maxilla and mandible (upper and lower jaws) began to dissolve. The mastoid (bone behind his right ear), his occipital (where the skull and cervical spine join) and the cervical spine also began to deteriorate. After two years of antibiotics through a central line in his chest (requiring him to come home from school for this treatment at lunch time each day, then return in the afternoon) and another biopsy, a correct diagnosis of Gorham's Syndrome, aka, Vanishing Bone Disease, was made.

As a preadolescent, Ryan spent a year and a half in halo traction, wherein a metal ring was screwed into his skull to stabilize the head and neck. The indention and scarring remained visible throughout his life, even after a fusion of his cervical spine just shy of his thirteenth birthday eliminated the necessity of the halo. The discomfort as well as his "odd" appearance should be obvious.

And how did his family deal with his halo? At Halloween they wrapped aluminum foil around the apparatus and Ry went Trick or Treating as an alien from Planet Kamukamuk. At Christmastime, he became a walking tree, complete with ornaments and battery pack for the lights, while at the press of a button his multicolored socks played **Jingle Bells, Santa Is Coming** and **Have a Merry Christmas**.

Ryan's life since age seven has been punctuated with illnesses that have included infections, pneumonias, meningitis, pleural effusions (fluid collection in the lining of the lung) and pneumothoraces (collapsed lungs). Treatments have ranged from intravenous (IV) antibiotics, hyperbaric oxygen chamber (five days per week for three months), daily injections, radiation and chest tubes.

I Loved a Boy

I marveled at Ryan's composure when bilateral chest tubes were inserted and he was tethered to a drainage reservoir the first summer I knew him. Ryan did not have cystic fibrosis (CF). I have witnessed children with chest tubes, usually those with CF. They have described the pain as akin to someone prying open a space between two ribs and inserting a garden hose! The pain persists with every movement of the body. This summer's hospitalization revealed that Ry's disease also affected a portion of his clavicle and a few ribs.

For half his life Ryan had been unable to take anything by mouth except for an occasional sip of fluids. His nutrition has never varied since age ten: eight or nine cans of Ensure, five regular, four with fiber, pumped each night into his gut through a jejunostomy (J) tube, with a gastric port (G tube) for continual release of stomach acids.

I recall the pathos of his fifteenth birthday, December 24, 1996 while an inpatient at Children's Hospital. Mom had made him a "cake" --- constructed of cans of Ensure decorated with ribbons and topped with candles. He could not blow out the candles due to the inability to purse his lips to exhale with sufficient force. No matter, they couldn't be lighted because he was on oxygen.

To provide a parade of "pity parties" would have been met with icy resistance. While living each day under the specter of a rare and unpredictable disease, Ryan dealt with his adversities with quiet courage, equanimity, enterprise, iron-willed determination and an outrageous sense of humor.

His voice was his computer and I have retained much of what he had to say. He loved to take the personality tests that frequent the Internet. Below are some of his mid-teen answers to one such instrument.

Q. Name given at birth?
A. Baby Boy.

Q. Nickname?
A. Nick.

Q. Hometown birthplace?
A. The hospital.

Q. Favorite salad dressing?
A. I'd rather see Salid un-dressing.

Q. Have you ever gone skinny dipping?
A. No, but I've never been fat dipping either.

Q. Do you make fun of people?
B. Only the stupid ones.

Q. Have you ever been convicted of a crime?
A. Not yet.

Q. Your first car?
C. Matchbox red Ferrari.

Q. Car you drive now?
A. Matchbox red Ferrari.

Q. Favorite foods?
A. Vanilla Ensure.

Q. Do you get along with your parents?
A. Only if they give me money.

Q. Favorite family game?
A. Hop on pop.

Q. What do you look for in the opposite sex?
A. Big boobs.

Q. Say one nice thing about the person who sent this e-mail to you?
A. ummm... he has a cool bum leg.

Q. Person you sent this to that is least likely to respond
A. Anyone who has any decency to stop these stupid e-mail things.

Once Ry was diagnosed, his activities were eliminated or restricted. The rambunctious kid with the squeaky voice and active mouth had to change. Ry on his Big Wheel. Ry on roller blades. Ry at age six grounded to his bedroom for jumping out of the second story window and then almost immediately knocking at the front door innocently seeking readmission to the house.

No more running, no more biking, no more schoolyard play. Wrestling, a favorite activity with his brother, had to cease. No basketball, baseball, soccer or any other activity in which he could be jostled. The transition from the running, jumping, sliding, yelling, rowdy, muscle kid in the neighborhood to a sedentary observer was made without a murmur.

To his Aunt Cathy, Ryan confided two premises of his personal philosophy:
1. It is wrong when a person is feeling badly, to make others feel bad.
2. It's not what you do in life, but how you handle what you do in life.

He modified his behavior, but not his attitude, which was one of the elements endearing him to me. He was strong-willed, sensitive, considerate, resolute, structured and clever. Early on, I am sure under the tutelage of big brother Chad, he cultivated a "love for the ladies."

Ryan's academic career is as remarkable as is his medical history. Due to multiple hospitalizations, he ventured into Stevenson High School in Sterling Heights as a part-time sophomore in the fall of 1997. He had not been in school full time since sixth grade. In the intervening years, a succession of teachers who came two hours per <u>week</u> taught him as a homebound. Ryan asserted, "I taught myself."

In high school he was observed walking alone down the halls with head bowed, according to Mr. Gene Collins, a school counselor. "We have to get this boy involved," the assertive and acerbic Collins said. For the remainder of his high school career, Ryan became an active participant in a volunteer club called S.O.S. (Students Offering Service). Collins even cajoled him into giving the invocation two years in a row at the school's annual charity appreciation dinner attended by some five hundred guests and supporters. For Ryan to agree to this, with his dislike for public speaking stemming from his difficulty in articulating clearly enough to be understood, was a tribute to the high regard he had for Mr. Collins.

"English II - A, Accounting I - A, Chemistry - A, Algebra 2 - B+, Business Law - B+" read his eleventh grade second semester report card. On one of the many occasions when I was at the house to pick him up for a weekend at Chalfonte, I noticed two photos of him on the kitchen counter. Ryan posed as if he were in a police lineup -- one a frontal view, the other a profile. I gulped to hold back tears of pride. Rather than jailhouse numbers, what he was holding at his chest was his certificate of induction into the National Honor Society. In June 2000, he graduated from high school, Magna Cum Laude.

Chapter 2: Chalfonte House

There was a leap in the growth of our relationship when Ry was fourteen and first invited to Chalfonte House. But let him tell the story.

The following documentation is from an e-mail uncovered when Ry's brother, Chad "broke the code" to his computer after his death. Less than a year before he died, Ryan had chronicled his five-year relationship with Chalfonte and me, to his friend, Devin Elsey.

...Anyway, so here goes the whole story of how I got involved with the priest that I go "up north" with, and the group of friends that accompany us. (You might want to go to the bathroom and get a drink and a snack, cuz you'll be here for awhile) :-} (smirk)

... then one evening, I'm lying in my bed watching TV. In walks this tall bald guy, with a white goatee, wearing a suit, holding (what I thought was) a suitcase. He says to me "Are you Ryan Giannini?" And I say, "yes". Now at this point I'm a little intimidated, cuz this guy looks like he means business. Then he says, "My name is James L. Meyer, and I want to be your AGENT!"

...and he told me who he was, and how he has a place up north that he takes kids every now and then. He said that most of the kids have cystic fibrosis (referred to as "CFers") or a type of bone cancer. But up at the house, you'd never know anyone had any kind of sickness. Then he asked me if I'd ever like to go. I told him "sure" but I think I only said that out of hesitation, and to be nice. I mean, here's this old priest guy who wants

14

to take me and some other guys I don't even know up to his house somewhere up north.

... I think we bonded pretty good that night. If I only knew what I was getting into.... :-} (smirk)

I recall picking up Ryan for his first Chalfonte adventure. It coincided with the day he had received a letter --- which he read with satisfaction, passing it on to his mother who passed it on to me. The letter was from their church's food pantry thanking him for a $185 donation. When first I had heard about Ryan's Store at Ford Hospital, I thought that he had grossed a couple of hundred bucks.

"$185 DONATION!" I queried, "Ryan, how much did you gross?"

"$2,000," was his reply.

"What the hell," I shouted, "YOU ARE A SCAMMER."

That nickname identified him for the rest of his life. Or as Ryan had stated in his e-mail to Devin: "... and I told him about $2,000, with a smile ... He went nuts! ... And right then and there, he gave me the nickname that has stuck ever since."

It will be important in subsequent chapters to recall the significance of Chalfonte in Ryan's life and relationships. Continuing his narration:

Now once we got into town he told me, "Okay, now find the house."

I was like, what the heck! I've never been here before.

"Four Friendships"
Jon Piercey. Jimeyer, Tim Burgess, Ryan Giannini

Scott Brinkman and Cheri Giroux
on their wedding day at Chalfonte

How am I supposed to know where the house was?"
(He does that to all 'Chalfonte Rookies.' There are tons
of traditions that come with knowing this guy.)

But lucky for me there were two other kids in the car.
He made them find the house too. One of the kids made
the mistake of saying 'that one.'

So Jimeyer said, "Okay, get out and knock on the door,
see if it's the house." And the kid actually did it! Lucky
for him no one was home. Anyway, we eventually got
to the house.

...For this weekend though, we stayed downstairs cuz
there was a family renting upstairs.

That weekend, I made four friendships that have only
gotten stronger through the years. One with a kid
named Tim (Burgess), who has osteosarcoma (bone
cancer). (Usually leads to having a prosthesis in your
leg or an amputation.) Another was a kid named Jon
'Piecey.' His real name is Piercey, but for some reason
he forgot how to spell his name when he wrote it in the
concrete porch behind the house.

Another friendship was with one of the 'councelers'
(sic) for the weekend, Scott (Brinkman). ... Well
anyway, the councelers really don't do much, except
maybe plan a few outings. Scott ended up moving to
Vermont with his soon-to-be wife, so I don't get to see
him that much any more.

And the last friendship I made was with Jimeyer...

"Moms and Munchkins Weekend" at Chalfonte
on a warm June afternoon

Chapter 3: More About Chalfonte House.

"And he (Jimeyer) <u>even</u> lied in church!" Chad exclaimed to his family upon returning from Ryan's funeral.

Though this book is a true story, in a few instances I have been "loose with the truth." Msgr. Francis X. Canfield, my English teacher in fourth year high school, admonished us with a twinkle in his eye, "Never let the truth stand in the way of a good story."

"Factual" stories, be they within families or friends, turn into legends, gaining elaboration with subsequent tellings. I will make every effort to identify the legends.

Chad was referring to my response to the pastor's request to tell the congregation what a "Chalfonte" is. This was prior to my homily at Ryan's "Mass of Resurrection" funeral service.

"In the twelfth century, deep in the forests of France," I began. (Smiles lit up the faces of those persons in the pews 'in the know.')...

> there was a region ruled for four centuries by a succession of benevolent kings. Even under a feudal system, the people of the land were happy and contented for hundreds of years. It was a "Shangri-La". The realm was called "Chal-font" or "Fountain of Life, Beauty and Goodness". Discovery by outsiders in the sixteenth century destroyed the kingdom and the people's tranquil way of life.

It is at this point, if I want people to know the reality, I will coach a veteran Chalfonte kid to pipe up with, "Jimeyer, isn't Chalfonte the name of the street in northwest Detroit on which you grew up?"

Now I ask, which version do you prefer?

The agenda at Chalfonte House for a weekend or a week varies little. No formal counseling or "intensives," unless requested on an individual basis, which often happens. One of my talents is bringing people together, stepping back, and letting things take their course. The benefits that occur result from the interaction of the Chalfonte Kids among themselves, irrespective of sex or age.

For males and mixed groups, backgammon and euchre (a card game) hold center stage as Chalfonte House activities. Courtesy of John Edward Welbank Searchfield IV and Ginny Smith, husband and wife from Calgary, Alberta, Canada, "Gangster" has come to the after-dinner table as a major group enterprise.

Girls and women have a different agenda. They plan. 2006 marked the fifteenth anniversary of Women's Weekend. This group consists of women with cystic fibrosis, cancer or other diseases, plus surviving siblings and supporters.

"Jimeyer we have four requests for our anniversary," they informed me.
1. Gourmet chefs.
2. Use of the pools and health spa at the Grand Traverse Resort.
3. Limousine service.
4. Massages at the house."

Thanks to "angels", all four requests were fulfilled at no expense to Chalfonte. Ann Marie "Grytz" Roberts quipped after "Antonio" (not his real name) had plied his craft as a massage therapist, "I'm leaving my husband."

A Women's Weekend
Back row: Debbie Ajini, Lori Fortino Franklin, Carol Carney,
Maureen Feighan-Kurth, Cathy Mellas
Middle row: Jimeyer, Carla Vollmer, Cheri Giroux, Linda
Thomas
Front row: Ann Marie Roberts, Bonnie Sweet, Pam Schuler

On a more serious note, Carla Vollmer, who has battled
cancer for over twenty years, wrote in the guest
book:

> Every year I leave Women's Weekend and
> Chalfonte House with great appreciation and more
> inner strength... You (Jimeyer) have never made me
> sob as long as I have known you! I really can't put
> into words what I feel. But I will say that I am so
> touched and honored by your words and symbolism.
> For that, I will never forget.

Rebekah Timlin Kaplan Meddles, age twenty-five, whose

husband died of cystic fibrosis after eighteen months of marriage, summarized:

> This is my home... and it is so hard to be away the rest of the year. The desert (she then lived in New Mexico) will never compare to Chalfonte House --- It will always be in my heart no matter where I am in the world.

No more incisive testimonial can be imagined than that of Matthew Gulker, then six years old on his initial stay at Chalfonte. The first night in the house he volunteered to his mother: "Mommy, I feel that God is in this place." Indeed.

I am not above subterfuge. Early in my ministry at Children's Hospital, I learned that card and board games are effective entrees into the life and heart of the most wary child. The religion card was rarely played. The patient's personal pastor met denominational needs.

My "M.O." (Modus Operandi or Manner of Operating) is to teach kids how to play backgammon and euchre. When they reach a self-determined confidence level, they are on their own. Thereafter I take money from them. (Gotta pay the mortgage!) Of course I would never violate laws forbidding unauthorized gambling in public places such as hospitals. There we play for "units" --- redeemable upon discharge.

Being a yoga practitioner and an admirer of Zen, I instruct my backgammon protégés in the subtle art of alpha (mind control). The purpose is to have the needed pips emerge on the face of the rolled dice. Am I sensing disbelief among some readers? I point you to the persistent plentitude of my "duck," the container holding my coins for gambling.

With the eloquence of an honor's graduate at Dexter

(Michigan) High School, Matt Baker has recounted his
experience. Matt was a CFer and Chalfonte Kid who died
on July 31, 1995 at age eighteen, two months after his high
school graduation. Matt writes:

> His (Jimeyer's) philosophy is that if you think it, it will
> happen. I first encountered Alpha on the backgammon
> board Jim brought with him one year to camp[1] I had
> never played before, so Jim was teaching me as we
> went along. In hindsight, I realize that was the only
> reason I was winning that particular game, but I was
> winning, so naturally I was happy.
>
> The game was a close one, but I began to pull away as I
> was bearing off well. Jim caught up as he usually does,
> and he put himself in a position to steal victory from the
> murky depths of defeat (sorry, couldn't help it). Thing
> was, he had to roll doubles to do it. Not just any
> doubles, these had to be high doubles.
>
> Undaunted, Jim shakes up the dice, drops one out of his
> cup. The six dots looking back up at him made his left
> eyebrow pop up with excitement. "Alpha." The word
> came out with such confidence I should have known
> what to expect. "What's that?" I asked. He explained it
> as I did earlier. "Can you say double sixes, baby?" I
> think he knew he was going to win. I didn't have it
> figured out until the other six hit the board.
>
> I probably wouldn't have written about that game had
> that been the only time Jim ever beat me with Alpha.
> Unfortunately it has happened several times, which
> leads me to believe that either Jim really does have

---

[1] Onkoi Benek, the Michigan camp for persons with cystic fibrosis
where I staffed from 1986 until it closed in 1996.

23

magic or that Catholic priests aren't above using trick dice. I'm leaning towards the former.

My didactic skills made a lasting impression upon Ryan, as he related to Devin years later.

I learned how to play euchre for the first time. I had no idea how to play! Jimeyer said he would help me, so I let him. Big mistake! On one of the hands, I was about to lay down a card, and I guess it was the wrong one, because his hand reached from behind me, slapped the card out of my hand, sending it flying across the room and said "NNNOOOOOOOOOOO! Scared the crap out of me! lol (laugh out loud).

Oh, and when we play cards, it's always for money. There are some rules as to how much money is played for. You play for dimes until you are sixteen. Once you are sixteen, you play with quarters "for the rest of your life." The losing team has to pay the winning team one "unit" for the game, one "unit" for the difference in the scorecards, and one 'unit' for any euchre they made. So if you're not careful, you can lose a few bucks on a game. And all of your money must be kept in some kind of "duck" (container to hold money). He calls it that cuz he has a ceramic mallard duck that splits in two to hold his money. So we played all night basically.

Ryan continues to Devin:
On Saturday, everyone went for a tour of Chateau Chantal which is a winery that Jimeyer is on the board of. Guess he had to replenish his stock or something. ☺ (smiley face) Then we went to the Elk Rapids Sportsmen's Club, where we got to shoot a few different guns at some targets. (I was a little hesitant about using them, cuz I mean, guns are bad. But as long

as it's not hurting anyone...) that was pretty fun.

We came back for a very nice dinner, complete with pie for dessert. You never leave the table hungry at that place, I'll tell ya. ...Oh, one of the other traditions is this --- whatever isn't eaten at dinner the night before, is breakfast the next morning. So that's a part of the reason why no one is ever hungry after dinner, cuz they don't want to eat it for breakfast. ☺

"Here's a priest who gambles, drinks and swears (a little) but he's still a priest. And he's really cool! Knowing that he gives all his time to kids just really inspired me...."

I try to instill some virtues to accompany my vices of "gambling, drinking and swearing (a little)". I am a big fan of involving townspeople as "angels" to satisfy some needs I am unable or reluctant to meet. For example, if a neighbor has provided a meal, I require each of us to write a few words of gratitude in a thank you card. Ryan's comments are classic: Something like... "I cannot begin to describe how good your lasagna was." This from a teen who has not taken food by mouth since age ten.

Snipe Hunting
Jim Binkley, Aarin Green, Dexter Solis, Eddie Wild and Kenny
Wallace (in chair)

Chapter 4: The Snipe Hunt

Matt Baker continues.

The entire week had been fun. We had gone to a fair, seen some classic cars, you know --- male-bonding stuff. So it didn't seem out of the ordinary when Jim suggested we go gather up some tools and try and catch some snipe. 'Snipe?' None of us had any clue what they were. Jim laid it all out for us. How snipe were little birds, and how we had to get permits to catch them, and who we could see to help us.

All this seemed strange to me, but this was Jim here and he wouldn't go through all this trouble just to make us look silly, would he? Our night began with us getting our permits, and then we went to a few of Jim's friends to see what we could learn about the finer points of snipe entrapment.

"I presume you have instructed these young persons concerning the rules of snipe hunting?" Dan Williams admonishes me when the group approaches his doorway. I mutter a reply. "And have you apprised them of the bounty on red-eyed snipe as well as the catch-and-release rules for the green-eyed?"

The State of Michigan vehicle in Dan's driveway lends credibility. We block the rookies from viewing the complete emblem which reveals "Boiler Inspector" beneath the logo. The form on a clipboard awaiting signatures of participants adds authenticity to Dan's presentation. The kids never read the paper they are signing, and so the "URBing Fooled" in the invoice box escapes them.

Rianna Baker, niece of Matt Baker, signs the "Tree of Life" during Moms and Munchkins Weekend

We prep the kids by visits to other Elk Rapids homes where the locals tell of current snipe hunting conditions. "They seem to be feeding on Cheerios," one source confided. Another provided sandwich bags filled with crushed ice, "to stroke their bellies and settle them down upon capture," we're informed.

By far the most creative information came from Charlie Williams, a retired high school counselor and Dan's dad. "I'm afraid the hunting has not been going well," he drolled. I braced myself for what was coming next. "Seems like there's been too many 'blur snipe.'" I bit my lip till it almost bled. "And, and, what are blur snipe, Charlie?" I stammered? "Welllllllllllllll, they go by so fast ... they're just a blur!"

Matt Baker picks up on our adventure,
> I stayed in the car with Jim because he had a cast on his foot and thusly didn't walk that well. It was in this car that the real bullhockey began to fly. Jim was filling my ear with interesting snipe facts and I ate up every one. He had me seeing things that weren't even there. Jim even had me get out of the car to investigate a possible snipe nest. I got down on all fours trying to see something that hadn't been there all night and certainly wasn't about to show up now...

Ryan was fuming when he returned from his hunt. Middle kids don't like to be "had". His revenge was swift and sweet. It had been drizzling when we left the kids at the snipe-capturing site. "I'm sick," he faked, "and I think I have a fever." "What the crap!" I thought in alarm. I'm familiar with cystic fibrosis and able to predict how CFers might feel, but what do I know about "Gorham's Syndrome?" What does anyone, including doctors?

I helped ease Ryan into the vibrating chair with the built-in heater (my chair!). I catered to him with the concern I reserve for the dying. And he milked it for about three hours before announcing that he had felt just fine.

And to Devin: "Then after that, it was time for snipe hunting! That was truely (sic) an experience. I probably would have liked it better, but it started raining a little while we were out there..."

What he didn't admit to Devin was that two other rookies, Chris Helmrich and Margaret Olstyn, instead of hunting snipe, were making lovey-dovey on the nearby bench while he sat by himself "unattached."

"I knew all the time it was just a fake," proclaimed Kris Matson at the end of the night. "Sure you did, Kris," Dan Timlin, a fellow rookie who bit the bait, countered. "And that's why you stood in the middle of the woods for half and hour with a fly swatter in one hand while holding up a bottle of minty-fresh mouthwash with the other."

Dan Williams joined us at the house afterwards to congratulate the novice hunters and declare them Master Snipers henceforth and forever. The tone was not of mockery but affirmation for those who reached another plateau of Chalfonte expertise. Williams concluded with the sagest comment of all: "Who's to say there are no snipe?"

From his first, what became Ry's mantra shines from each of his many entries in the guest book. His final sentence reads: "And, as always, I will look forward to any return visits to Chalfonte House."

My own occasional comments from that weekend are as

telling: "Ryan the Scammer is such a wonderful companion to either young or adult Chalfonte Kids. I only wish he wouldn't pick on me...."

Chapter 5: Teen Rent-A-Kids

I refer to the children as "rent-a-kids." As I explain to parents, "I don't have the courage you have to buy them --- so I just rent them. Always a grandparent, never a parent -- I did it the right way."

"What a marvelous man you must be," experienced parents reply when I declare that I prefer to rent teenagers.

"Rent?" they retort, "Hell, I'll GIVE you mine for free." One parent gifted me with a hand-painted plaque that now graces the kitchen wall at Chalfonte: "*Raising Teenagers is Like Nailing Jell-O to a Tree.*"

"You don't understand," I protest. "I prefer teens to preteens for very selfish reasons. Unlike preadolescents who never seem to tire, teenagers <u>sleep</u> in the morning. And the morning is my prime time. A pot of coffee, a dish of fruit and tranquil reverie."

I am content to let the teens sleep as long as they like --- unless we have a planned morning activity. In the latter circumstance a problem emerges. How to get them up and moving? Ever respectful of the exigencies of early morning arousal, (I am scrupulous about never embarrassing anyone) years ago I patented a foolproof procedure. Kudos to the gravelly tones of Fats Domino. Prior to Ryan's description (below), accept as a premise that I am no dancer. Hence the following is a frequent but never a pretty picture.

Right about 10 a.m., while everyone was sleeping, all of a sudden we hear the CD player blasting this song,

Blueberry Hill. I'm like, what the heck! After a few notes, Jimeyer charges into the room yelling 'Good morning my lovelies!' and then he proceeds to take the covers off of everyone (luckily everyone had something on), pulls everyone up by their arms and starts dancing with them to this crazy song! I quickly learn not to sleep in later than 10...or else I'll be the victim of this wake-up call!

YESSSSSSSSSSS! Once again, "old age and treachery overcomes youth and skill". On subsequent occasions, the Pavlovian response is so effective with the veterans that I need only touch the stereo knob and they are vertical with feet on the floor. However, I hope the Roman brothers, Nathan and Sir Charles, do not read this. In these latter years, the escalation of my arthritis and their teen-age frames, each between 250 and 350 pounds, have stymied me.

In his next remarks, I am "damned by faint praise." Ry fails to capture the hours I spend in preparing the right texts and music tailored to each Sunday Morning Gathering. Casting his remarks in optimal light, I choose to conclude that he doesn't want to sound too pious to Devin. My theory is well founded because in latter years, Ry assisted me in preparing the service by providing music from his impressive collection.

He writes to Devin

> After everyone was up, we gathered in the living room for Sunday service. There's no reading readings like how there is at church. It's more like a few passages from the bible that fit into some kind of theme he picks. And along with the passages, Jimeyer plays a few songs (on a tape player) that he put together that go along with the service. After that, we all say the Our Father.

Dexter Solis feels the joy of accomplishment

When that's done, Jimeyer takes a plate with a piece of bread on it from the makeshift altar (a TV table with a candle, and a cross on it) and turns to the person next to him, and just says a few words about that person. ("It was great spending this time with you, I wish you luck, hope things go okay..."). Then he breaks off a piece of bread, and gives it to the person next to him. Then that person does the same for the person next to him, and so on until everyone has some. After that we talk about the weekend, and then it's time for breakfast."

I don't give a sermon. Our dialogue revolves around the theme and the readings. I recall after one teen service, the only sibling and sister of a CFer took me aside to thank me. With tears in her eyes, she confided, "I have never before been able to say publicly how much my brother means to me and how much I admire him".

I am bemused as I recall fifteen-year-old Dexter Solis at one of the services. He not only copes with cystic fibrosis, but also autism. Dexter is direct but without a surly bone in his body. Asked how he liked the service, he deadpanned: "The bread's too dry." Since that time, we use honey on the bread. I don't think Jesus would object.

My ease with this ecumenical approach stems from the way I practice chaplaincy. Ministry is divided according to medical specialty rather than religion or lack thereof. For example, at Hutzel Hospital, (now Hutzel Women's Hospital) where I directed pastoral care for almost thirty years, I chose gynecologic oncology, orthopedics and intensive care as my areas of activity. My chaplain colleague, of a different religion, ministered to moms and babies. Hence when a Catholic, Episcopal or Lutheran mom requested baptism, she performed it. When a Baptist or other mom asked for a dedication or prayer, she satisfied the request.

Chapter 6: Touch

The most profound life-lesson that I learned in hospital ministry was the value of <u>touch.</u> I did not grow up in a "touchy" family. I don't ever remember my dad touching me in love. For compliance maybe, not in love. I learned touch at the bedside of dying children. They often feel valueless and less than human because of imperfection and the disappointment they are to those they love because of their sickness and dying. If one is unwilling to embrace these, one will be far less effective. If one is unwilling to hold a grieving mother or a disconsolate father to one's breast in prolonged embrace, the separation is telling. A handshake with words of sympathy doesn't cut it. Moments ago I opened my annual Christmas card from Rick and Pam Pope. "We'll never forget you, Father Jim," they penned. I have not seen the Popes since I buried their newborn, Daniel Joseph--- fourteen years ago.

"One of the greatest indictments of American society," I railed from the pulpit on more than one occasion, "is our difficulty with touch"! My reference is exemplified in a TV program called *Teach, Don't Touch*. Therein lawyers retained by public schools admonish teachers that under no circumstances should they ever touch a child. What duplicity in a culture reeking with sexual innuendo from every pore and where pornography and perversion are leading cottage industries! I am not so naive as to ignore the litigiousness of American society. The tragedy of a touchless society is that it is an aberration of human nature. Kids should be taught about "good touch" and "bad touch," but "no touch"?

Recognizing the awful reality of the pedophilia scandals of Catholic priests which have become public, many of my colleagues have suspended their practice of embracing children upon entering and exiting church. For my part, I am overwhelmed by the natural unmitigated love, acceptance and innocence of the little ones who gather round me for mutual hugs after my liturgies.

In the Bible, the book to which I pledge my allegiance, I read: "Jesus touched." In the tenth chapter of the gospel of Luke (Lk 10: 30-34) Jesus was in dialog with lawyers (like myself). In making the point about who is one's neighbor he told the following story:

> There was a traveler going down from Jerusalem to Jericho who fell prey to robbers. The traveler was beaten, stripped naked and left half-dead. A priest (like myself) happened to be going down the same road. The priest saw the traveler lying beside the road, but passed by on the other side. Likewise there was a Levite who came the same way. This one too saw the afflicted traveler and passed by on the other side. But a Samaritan (a stranger) who was taking the same road also came upon the traveler and filled with compassion, approached the traveler and dressed the wounds, pouring on oil and wine. The Samaritan put the wounded person on a donkey, went straight to an inn and there took care of the injured one.[2]

The message that it was the priest who passed by the ugly, bruised, bloodied and dying body is not lost on me. The times I've "passed by" haunt me --- as much as the times I've stopped to offer solace bring me consolation.

---

[2] *"**The Inclusive New Testament**,*"* Priests for Equality pp 119-120

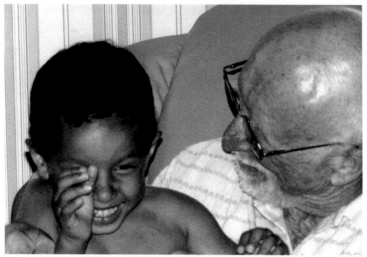

Jimeyer embraces Nicholas Franklin

Jeff Shorkey helped me learn to do it right. He called me to his bedside one November evening. Jeff at age thirteen had chosen to die at home. The metastases of his osteosarcoma was evident. One tumor on the back of his head had grown to the size of half a tennis ball, while others on his abdomen and inside his cheek were tormenting him.

Jeff's older brother, Steve, had been released from the intensive care unit where he was being treated for schizophrenia and end stage kidney failure. He sat staring from the couch, on oxygen like his dying brother. The oldest sibling, Dave, is there as well, along with his wife Sara. Al and Karyn, their parents, are by the bed in the middle of the living room. Today is his mom's birthday. Jeff struggles to sign a card.

When I sit down beside him, Jeff instructs me to place my hand over his heart. Then he places his hand atop mine. "I love you very much," he whispers as he looks me straight in the eye. "I love you too, Jeff," I mutter in return. What a transformation! Six months before he was inveighing against his disease. "I'm just now growing up; life is just beginning; why the f _ _ _ is this happening to me," he raged. He had little truck with pious preaching. He insisted on being left alone and untouched, throwing things and people out of his hospital room.

This evening he asks about heaven and what awaits him. He asks for prayer. I am grateful his pain is controlled. After an hour and a half with my hand on his heartbeat, his hand pressed against my own, he dismisses several others saying their presence is "too much" for him. I rise to leave. He motions me back into the chair. "Don't go Jim... I will never see you again." For an additional hour and a half we talk or are silent, hands resting on each other's over his heart - over his life - within his love. I finally bid farewell.

I speak with an abundance of ignorance on this matter when I assert the pleasure bond in sexual intercourse that brings ecstasy and fulfillment, pales when measured against the intimacy forged upon the anvil of pathos and vulnerability with one close to death, especially a child. When one is permitted, even bidden, to participate at this time of ultimate transition everyone makes but once, I am awed at the privilege. It has been mine over and over again. This may sound strange, but I savor the honor as "the hart ever thirsting for renewing waters"[3]. I left Jeff's side that evening, the eve before he died, feeling to the core of my viscera what it is to be fulfilled as a man, a father and a lover.

For years I have beaten kids. I admit, I'm dang good at it. In the CF community we call it "P& PD" (percussion and postural drainage) or "CPT" (chest physiotherapy). The pounding is euphemistically called "clapping." It may be performed in nine different positions on chest and upper back, for up to forty- five minutes, as often as three times daily, in order to help expel the thick mucus lodged in CFers lungs. After these intrusions, I would often hug the child or teen. I learned the rudiments of neck and back massage. Frequently I would "treat" them to a massage after their pounding. Advances in respiratory medicine have substituted other methods of airway clearance. That's sad, for what is lost is the intimacy of touch.

Robbie McNeilage was a handsome, smart, self-assured sixteen-year-old when we traveled alone to my cottage for a weekend. Adolescents as a rule don't like to be touched. He surprised me when he allowed me to do his therapy. Afterwards he quipped: "You know, Jimeyer," I don't

---

[3] Refer to Psalm 42, **The Old Testament**

allow anyone to do my PD except the professionals at the hospital --- and my mother. And you do it better than she." I was chagrined later when we started the week at CF camp. "Jimeyer," he cautioned, "don't even offer to do my PD." When I entered the lodge and observed the comely blond female staffer pounding him, I understood. "*Lemonade out of lemons.*" God, I love these kids!

I Loved a Boy

Jimeyer and Andrew Peter Morsches

Chapter 7: Body Image

We alternate between incorporating and overcoming the lessons and experiences of our childhood. I recall a greeting card sent me years ago by my older sister. "Want to have a real scare at Halloween?" the front announced. The inside message read: "Just think how much as an adult you act like your mother!"

Attribute it to religious, cultural or social upbringing -- it doesn't matter which. Growing up in my home in the thirties and forties with two providing parents, and an older sister and brother; bodily functions such as elimination, let alone sex, did not occur. If they did, it was only behind closed and locked doors. You kept your "privates" covered --- and they were not to be mentioned. As far as I understood it, the morality of peeing behind the garage was no different than adultery.

The word "pregnancy" was not used when I was around. One day a baby sister "arrived" at my house. I was almost nine years old. I participated in her care. The anatomy questions that might have surfaced from diapering were lost beneath my pouting for having to "take care of her."

Some parents including my mother assert, "I love all my children equally." This has not been my experience but I am at a loss to understand the reasons for the hierarchy of my love and affection. Three persons stand high above the others, each with different relational dynamics.

First is Andrew Peter Morsches from Arlington Virginia. Our relationship was as son to a father. A physical, intellectual, and artistic Adonis, Andrew Peter was killed

on his bicycle on September 6, 1988 while away at college
--- but who remembers the date? (Sardonic smile) It was
the most desolate day of my life.

For Ryan, who became second, our relationship was as
mentor to student. He was like an avid though
discriminating fledgling waiting to be nourished.

Artistic, precocious, outspoken and independent describe
Matt Schmidt, whom I had befriended years before during
his hospital admissions away from his home in Alpena,
Michigan, a four-hour drive from Detroit. He remains third
in my affection. Though old enough to be his father, the
paradigm of my love for Matt was as an intimate peer. I
was a priest in my mid-forties living in a two-bedroom
apartment in a housing project adjacent to the Detroit
Medical Center and Children's Hospital of Michigan.
"Why shouldn't I have the experience of having a teen live
with me? It is common to the majority of men," I
counseled myself when Matt asked if he could move in.

I learned much from Matt in the better part of a year we
lived together. I learned that, like the hydra, chronic disease
has multiple faces of evil that continually bite you in the
ass. Matt at nineteen had surpassed by four or five years the
life expectancy of a person with cystic fibrosis. I embraced
him when he returned home one evening dejected and in
tears, a rare posture for him. His first serious love had jilted
him. She confessed she could not allow herself to fall in
love with one who was going to die prematurely. I don't
blame her. Nor did Matt.

Matt died at age twenty-one, the day after his marriage to
Vikki Brown Kocielo. I performed the ceremony at his sick
bed at Children's Hospital. Next day I caught hell for doing
so by the president of the hospital. When summoned to his

office I rebutted: "You couldn't buy that kind of human interest coverage taking up a quarter of the front page of Sunday's edition of the Detroit Free Press! What the hell is your problem?"

"Jim, he married one of our nurses," he replied. "That indicates there has been fraternization between our patients and the staff." I walked out of his office shaking my head and muttering, "I don't believe this."

This is but a bit of the baggage burdening the backpack borne by those afflicted with CF and other wasting diseases. CFers banter among themselves about their skinny "cystic legs".

Artificial enzymes and feeding tubes are no substitute for normal nutrition. Often these children are smaller than average and delayed in their maturation. Ryan was five foot two and one-half inches in height and weighed one hundred and fifteen pounds at twenty years of age. His mother contends that he should have been over six feet tall.

Hours of daily therapy, thus impatient peers can't wait; discolored teeth (if teeth at all) and other remarkable disfigurements occasioning stares and finger pointing; incessant coughing, precluding attendance at a stage play or the symphony.

"*Bigger is better*" is false. Right. But tell that to the twenty-year-old woman who looks like she's eleven. And what high school junior has the self-confidence to be comfortable at the prom when her date is a seventeen year old boy who can pass for ten?

I recall the single open shower-room in the boy's dorm at Onkoi Benek, the CF camp I staffed for ten summers.

Seven-year-old through adolescent campers showered together with adult staff. All of us were buck-naked. We as staff insured that no attention was directed toward developmental differences even amidst the playful antics that prevailed. The unspoken affirmation of the kids was deafening. All of us and all of our parts come in a variety of sizes and contours, but we are no different, one from the other.

Fr. Edward Hays writing in ***Prayer Notes to a Friend*** (Forest of Peace Publishing) casts it in the context of spirituality: "Whenever you become conscious of your body while dressing or bathing, pray a wordless prayer that you will never desert your body, or any parts of it, for some artificial state of holiness."

Overcoming childhood inhibitions, I have championed the message with my kids that each and every part of their body is beautiful. None need bow to the bully of the marketplace by allowing it to dictate the acceptable teen figure. These kids, like Ryan, feel compelled to conceal an anatomy distorted by disease, surgery or medication. "You don't have to take your swim suit into the bathroom to change," I would challenge; "all of us have similar parts."

"Now here are some bathroom rules," I bellow to the rookies as we tour Chalfonte. "For sound ecological reasons, and because I am cheap and sewage is expensive, we follow the principle: 'If it's yellow, let it mellow, if it's brown, flush it down.'"

Up until 2001, we had only one bathroom for as many as ten boys and three staff, so the next rule was practical. "Consider the bathroom like a locker-room," I instructed. "Therefore, 'Knock, Don't Lock.' One kid might have to whizz, another shower, another wash his hands. It's okay to do so simultaneously. However, when you are using the 'library', you know, the porcelain receptacle that holds *National Geographic* on the back tank top, just shout 'library' in response to the knock at the door and your seclusion will be assured."

I respect the adolescent's need for privacy. The rules announced above have been followed as often in their breach as in their observance. Ryan insisted on bathroom isolation and locked the door. He was never chided for it, nor were others who did the same.

Years ago Ryan uttered words that resound in my head and today bring me sweet comfort: "Jimeyer, you have never treated me as different, you always treat me as unique."

Eight adolescents in this 15 year old Chalfonte photo, have cystic fibrosis. Six have died.

Chapter 8: Living with Chronic Illness

As Paul of Tarsus studied at the feet of the great Rabbi
Gamaliel, I kneel at the feet of these kids. The words of my
mouth sound anemic when I suggest that they are vessels
containing the knowledge and wisdom of how life is to be
lived. When Dan Kaplan, a CFer, was sixteen and he and I
were driving back from Chalfonte after a weekend together,
he inquired: "Jimeyer, are we different?" My knee-jerk
reaction was to say "No," so as not to suggest they are not
normal. Instead, my answer was, "Yes, you have a
dimension and a no-nonsense attitude toward life that the
rest of us can admire but not attain. You <u>live</u> what the rest
of us parrot -- namely 'One Day at a Time' --- lived to the
fullest."

In our society, cystic fibrosis is purported to be the number
one genetic killer of children and young adults. One out of
twenty Caucasian Americans is a carrier; one out of sixty
among African Americans. If two carriers marry and have
children, the odds are the same with every pregnancy. One
chance in four the child will have CF, one chance in four
she or he will not, and two chances in four she or he will be
a carrier. Unlike osteosarcoma which affects boys
predominantly, CF is not sexually selective.

When I began working with CFers in 1971, life expectancy
was age 15 or 16. In 2005, the mean age is touted as 36.8
years.

However, my ministry is with persons with greater
morbidity and excessive mortality because they are
hospitalized more often.

Simply described, CF is gunk in the lungs which impairs the ability to breathe. I assert: "We have a constitutionally guaranteed right to life --- but not to breathe --- because breathing is so fundamental". CFers can never take breathing for granted. Their thick secretions compromise functioning of other organs as well.

Years ago, someone e-mailed me the TOP TEN INDICATIONS THAT YOU MAY HAVE CF. No comment is necessary:

10 When you walk your pet turtle, you have trouble keeping up.

9 Horses follow you around because they think you are a salt lick.

8 The Smithsonian Institution offered to purchase your pill collection.

7 All your friends think your "blue lipstick" is way cool.

6 The local pharmacy named you "Customer of the Year."

5 You take a cab to your mailbox.

4 Your insurance agent tells you that crash test dummies have a better chance of getting life insurance than you do.

3 On your last birthday, you used a hair dryer to blow out the candles on your cake.

2 You got beat up by the Energizer bunny.

I Loved a Boy

1 The only vein you have left is the weather vane on
  your garage.

Many CFers are eager to participate in their school music
programs. They choose wind instruments. Debby Schuler,
a spit and vinegar CFer who died in 1996 at age twenty-
one, after a failed lung transplant, chose the tuba in her
high school marching band. As CFers cop an "in your face"
(pardon the expression) attitude toward breathing by
selecting wind instruments, Ryan, who did not have CF but
who couldn't eat, adopted a similar attitude toward edibles.
One of his hobbies was growing vegetables.

His mom narrates:

> I'd take Ry to choose which veggies he wanted to grow
> and we went to a different place each year. He would
> decide in which area of the garden they would go
> because each year he rotated them as he learned that
> from the master gardener. And he planted them himself.
> I bought him gloves to use but after trying them, he
> decided he would rather not use them and so he'd get
> his hands all dirty. He would also go out there every
> day and pull the weeds .... Ryan's great grandfather,
> who lived in Detroit, also grew a garden and would talk
> to Ry about their common interest and check out each
> other's gardens when each visited the other's house. ...
> (Ry) would venture out and pick his veggies in the
> same big white bowl and share them with family and
> friends. The year he was in the hospital for the whole
> summer it was tough for him to care for (his garden)....

Chapter 9: Traveling with School Marms

"No, Joan, you should not have any medical emergencies in the five hours it takes to pick up and drive the three boys to Chalfonte House," I say to my school principal friend and her teacher companion. "Don't be intimidated by Tim's baldness or Craig's amputation. They both have osteosarcoma, bone cancer, and are in treatment. Ryan has a rare disease called Gorham Syndrome also known as Vanishing Bone. They are thirteen, fifteen and fourteen respectively and are used to taking care of themselves."

As I hung up the phone, I realized there is an inverse proportion to my comfort level around sickness and disease and that of most other persons. However, I hadn't factored in the perversity of adolescent boys who can smell a novice like a hyena to a lion's kill. Nor could I predict their five-hour trip would take eleven. Understand the following account is hearsay from three very defensive sources, but this is how I heard the tale of: "Let the games begin!"

"Oh, oh we're sick!" moaned two of the three. "Stop the car, quick!" Joan swerved into the nearest respite and all three boys raced inside. Remaining in the front seat, Joan and Mary wrung their hands for several minutes, until they realized something was amiss. They glanced at the marquee of the establishment, *Hooters*, into which the boys had fled. Being dragged to the back seat by their ears, the boys protested: "No, no, we really had to go. We didn't see nuttin. Weeelllll........ there was some silverware on the floor next to that one lady. I thought it would be chivalrous to get down and pick it up for her," Ryan confessed.

Continuing the trip, the schoolmarms were lulled into

complacency by the well-behaved trio in the back. It was stop-and-go construction from south of Grayling onward. "But notice how friendly the people are up here," Mary observed. "So many honk their horns and wave at us." "Hi there," she waves back, again and again. It was three days later in cleaning out the back seat, that Joan noticed the bold, hand printed sign forgotten there. "Honk if You're Horny."

And on the return trip, injury was added to insult when all five in the car started laughing so hard they couldn't pull off their planned "medical emergency" scam, when the officer came back to the car with Joan's speeding ticket.

Some "Chalfonte Angels" flit in once or twice and flutter away. Others have staying power, like Barbara George, who for two decades has chosen doing house laundry as her mission. "Does the laundry lady at your house pick up the family laundry in a white Cadillac?" I challenge, as Barb drives up to the house. "You broke my machines," she once lamented in cheerful jest, "twenty-one loads -- that must be some kind of record"!

After their experience with the adolescents, Joan and Mary flitted and fluttered away, never to be heard from again.

Chapter 10: The Cat

Ry and I were traveling to Torch Lake. We both saw the cat running top speed toward us. Demonstrating my driving prowess, I sped up to zoom in front of the traversing feline. We heard, "thump, thump." My heart sank. Much to my relief, through the rear view mirror I thought I saw the cat tumble over twice before bounding off into the woods. I admitted that she might have only seven lives left. Ryan would have none of my recital.

Whenever conversations came close to the subject, Ry would apply the palm of his hand to any reverberating surface. "Thump Thump." Listeners knew what that meant and evil eyes were directed toward me. It didn't help that friends recalled my mantra: *The Only Good Cat is a Microwaved Cat.*" Or the bumper sticker I had longed for: "*Cat, the Other White Meat*".

I subscribe to my friend, Paul Hresko's bias. "Having a cat is like having a rude roommate."

Nor was it beneficial that in the compulsion to talk that ensues when one has been caught in an act of indiscretion, I blabbed to Ry that once I had hit a small deer --- perhaps a dog on another occasion. Well, also several slow-moving Detroit pigeons years ago.

Early next morning I entered the empty kitchen in hot pursuit of my morning cup of coffee. Yawning, stretching --- my eyes caught sight of a poster appended to the refrigerator door. "Jimeyer's Hit List" it blared in boyish letters. Arranged below, complete with check boxes were the following: "Tabby," "Rover," "Bambi" and "City

Pigeon," all marked. Then, waiting to be checked --
"skunk," "raccoon" and "Kenny's stuffed animal." Kenny
Wallace was another teen spending that week at Chalfonte.
He had the unenviable distinction of having ADHD and
Tourette's Syndrome accompanying his cystic fibrosis.

To paraphrase John 8:7: *"Let him without tire-tracks on the
backs of cats, cast the first stone."*

Ryan had created a game called "Bowling for Cats." Here
is how the game was played. Dad arranged Ry's empty
Ensure cans as ten pins at one end of the kitchen floor at
home. Then from the far end, Chad and his dad would wind
up and slide the "boarder kittens" into the pile to see how
many cans they could disrupt. Ry doubled over in mirth (it
was difficult for him to laugh, or cry, because of the
distortions of his facial anatomy) while Cindy walked away
in disgust. I have it on good authority that for catless
families the game works just as well with puppies.

I say "boarder cats" because one of the on-going ministries
of the Giannini family was to rehabilitate sick, abused and
abandoned animals for the Humane Society. The front of
their frig is smothered with photos of the animals they had
fostered. Willa became more than just another pretty
dogface; she is now a permanent resident.

Ryan's cavorting with animals goes back to preschool days
before he was sick. As school ended, no one had signed up
to take Ruffles, the guinea pig for the summer. Not only did
he care for her then, but also when September came, this
four-year-old brought her carrots and celery three times a
week. Teachers remarked about how attentive Ruffles was
when Ryan spoke to her. She did that for no one else. On
graduation day, Ryan was given Ruffles to keep. He was
very happy. And Ruffles lived with him far longer than

normal guinea-pig years.

Despite the tawdry cat tale told above, Ryan and his family were friends of animals. When informed of his death, the *Volunteer Voice* of the Michigan Humane Society published this blurb:

> In 1995, Ryan had talked his mother, Cindy, into volunteering with him at the Rochester Hills shelter, walking dogs and doing laundry. It wasn't long before Ryan talked Cindy into fostering animals from Rochester Hills and Detroit. Working together, they fostered nearly one hundred dogs, cats, puppies and kittens. Puppies were his favorites and Cindy recalls that foster pet number twenty seven was a special one. "That foster was a cruelty case with an embedded collar and let to live outside without shelter. Ryan formed a special bond with the dog, which we adopted and named Willa."

Chapter 11: The Train Trip

As the old bromide has it, *"It is not what you know, but who you know."* When one lives as long as I, with many and varied experiences, the network is far and wide. I am always on the lookout for someone who can help my kids.

Early in our relationship I learned that Ryan had a passion for passenger trains. Through my contacts, I procured our first rail adventure; a short trip from Flint to Plymouth, Michigan, traveling with a covey of teachers and safety persons. It was a didactic trip to demonstrate how frequently automobiles disregard railroad crossing signals and gates (very frequently). A TV camera had been mounted on the front of the engine and monitors installed in the passenger cars so we could see what the engineer would see. Ryan was enthralled. But the best was yet to come.

I have a thing about remembering kids' birthdays --- particularly thirteenth, sixteenth, eighteenth and twenty-first, which are significant life events. These are pertinent for CFers, who in the past frequently died before attaining many of these milestones.

I had wrapped Ryan's sixteenth birthday present in a huge three foot square box and cautioned him that this was to be a "twofer," Christmas being the day after his birthday. I insisted both his parents be present in my apartment for our gift exchange. When Ryan got to the bottom of the package he discovered a small, almost missed, envelope. Therein was a letter from a benefactor awarding him a train trip for two --- to whatever destination he desired. Recalling an article he had read with longing years before in one of his many train magazines, Ry selected the Rocky Mountaineer's exclusive "gold leaf" tour though the Canadian Rockies. I was chosen as his traveling companion.

It was more intimidating than I acknowledged to be handed a notarized, certified State of Michigan document entitled: DELEGATION OF AUTHORITY which read:

> We RICHARD GIANNINI and CYNTHIA GIANNINI of (address) do hereby authorize Fr. James Meyer to act in our place and stead during all times our son, RYAN GIANNINI is under his care, custody and control, more specifically, during the cross-country rail trip planned for (dates). FR JAMES MEYER is authorized by us to make any necessary medical, financial, transportation, lodging and over-all care decisions and/or arrangements concerning RYAN. We have the utmost trust and confidence in FR. MEYER and hereby entrust RYAN into his care.

I had invited sixteen year old Ryan to spend the night of June 3, 1998 alone with me in my apartment, as I had done with him and countless other boys on countless occasions over countless years. On this occasion, I wanted "to get an early start for a lengthy trip," commencing next morning at the Amtrak station in the shadow of the General Motor's building in the New Center area in Detroit.

Arriving at the station at seven next morning, I growled more in disbelief than anger: "Waddayamean you left one of your bags at the apartment!" I envisioned that at any moment the train would be pulling into the station --- and out again --- its stack belching the black and gray smoke I recalled from old movies. Whenever, as now, Ry was caught "with his hand in the cookie jar," he would put on

1998 U.S. – Canada Train Trip
Jimeyer and Ryan Giannini at age 16

his coy smirk and stand in front of you in silence. It was difficult to get upset when he charmed you with that look. Before tranquility returned and I realized we had time to retrieve the errant bag, I calculated how long it would take to drive to Union Station in Chicago to board train No. 7, *The Empire Builder* for the first major leg of our adventure.

"My name is Suzanne, and I will be your attendant," she said with practiced politeness as we boarded our sleeper en route from Chicago to Seattle. It's hard to look "cool" when both are inexperienced with Pullman cars ---- and so excited we can hardly breathe. Attendants are more than an amenity in cross-country rail travel. They are necessary to cobble together the berths and arrange the safety netting to prevent the upper-bunk person from crashing into the person beneath during the night.

As time for sleep arrived, Ry plugged his feeding pump into the only outlet which was in my bunk. Then he slipped into his spider web above me. I figured out that if I dangled my feet toward the door and didn't move much, I could accommodate most of my body on the tiny pallet and get some semblance of rest. I must have, for it was only the distant mournful wail of the train's whistle that awakened me. I lifted the corner of the curtain to daylight and the prairie. "Ryan, dig this," I called to the small mass stretching nearby.

I admit, my coordination leaves much to be desired, but manipulating toilet and shower, both juxtaposed in a tiny triangular crevice of the compartment, would challenge the most adroit. Ryan didn't even try --- saving his scented body for a shower in Seattle -- three days hence.

Havre, Montana, will remind me forever of my "Great Fall" --- off the platform. It was hard enough that it smashed both camera and my body. Only with assistance was I able to get up off the ground. Had I not, I envisaged Ryan, nose pressed against the inside windowpane, mouthing and waving -- "Bye, bye, my trip, good luck in Havre. God bless you" --- as the train sped away.

There are disadvantages to traveling with one who systematically sups at the trough of suffering. "Ryan, I hurt," I repeated one too many times. "Quit complaining," he retorted in exasperation. After all, my head and body were together without pins - and I could walk and I could talk and I could eat. "Well at least may I borrow some of your extra strength Excedrin?" I whimpered.

Years before I had learned to dodge the "sympathy" bullet from fourteen-year-old Trevor Banka, who had bone cancer. Thinking I was doing a favor advocating for another youngster with the same disease, I had asked Trev if he would talk to the kid. Trev, well on the pathway today toward becoming a pediatric orthopedic surgeon, was and is very empathetic. "Is he looking for sympathy?" Trev flashed back at me. "Well, ah, yes, maybe a little." Without hesitation he continued, "Tell him to look it up in the dictionary --- it's between shit and syphilis!" End of discussion, both with Trevor then and Ryan now. However Ry did share his pain meds.

As a priest in my late twenties I traveled with a good friend, Hugh Timlin, twelve years my junior. He used to be my altar boy. Now he is the father of seven adult children. Driving my Fiat 124 Sport Spider we had two rules: One - never drive the Interstate Highway, and two, never put the top up. Patrick, Hugh's younger brother gave us sage counsel that I observe to this day. When traveling with anyone in close physical proximity (as in a 124 Sport Spider, or in an adjacent bed) be certain to schedule time apart from each other --- or before the trip ends, there is likely to be a homicide or two.

Traveling with Ryan, Patrick's wisdom was "built in" due to our diverse sleeping habits. In short: Ry up late, Jimeyer up early. This had a bonus. I did something that was not my custom. I would spend time journaling while savoring my fruit and morning pot of coffee awaiting Ryan's resurrection.

We had both crashed early our first night at the Warwick of Seattle - me at 9 p.m., Ryan soon afterwards. In my reverie the next morning, I was content to listen to Ryan's subtle snore and the rhythmic drone of his Kangaroo (feeding pump). Both were sounds I would savor with satisfaction in subsequent days and nights we would spend together until his death.

Sausage and waffles, juice and milk, Blimpe's sub with fries, Mountain Dew and I think I'll have a pizza. You name it -- all were the same for Ryan --- day after day, week after week, year after year since he was ten years old. He could take nothing by mouth, except for an occasional sip of fluids. At bedtime, he would unpack nine cans of Ensure- five vanilla plain and four with fiber, arrange his syringes filled with medications, and begin his nocturnal feeding ritual through the jejunostomy tube in his gut. His run approximated ten hours. But his pump held only half the liquid, which meant awakening each and every night for a refill. Never a complaint.

To underscore Ryan's acceptance of his condition, in March of 2001, I was preaching a homily at Kensington Academy's Mass prior to its annual pancake breakfast. Ry was staying at my apartment. Prior to the Sunday service, our weekend had been filled with a Pax Christi peace conference and an amazing mind-games performer at the Gem Theatre in downtown Detroit.

The lesson for the Mass was the story of the Prodigal Son in the fifteenth chapter of Luke's gospel (Lk 15: 11-31). The synopsis is this: The younger son demands his inheritance, takes off and squanders it and while starving decides to return home to be treated as one of his dad's hired hands.

While preparing the sermon I got this brilliant idea to have Ryan say a few words about what it is like not to have food --- like the starving prodigal son, get it? In his direct style so endearing to me Ryan asks: "Do you want me to get them (the congregation) to feel sorry for me?" "No Ryan, not at all," I reply. "You are in a unique position to speak to what it is like not to have food. Address that issue." This is what he said:

> What does food mean to me? Well, since I have not had any for the past ten years, it does not mean too much to me. But I do miss it. I miss tasting all the different tastes. Sometimes, just smelling food, like pizza or popcorn, will bring the taste back to my mouth. I also see food as a time to get together with friends and family. I am welcome at the table, but it makes me feel strange watching everyone eat and not being able to join them.

I felt pride and satisfaction, not only for the rapt attention Ryan received at the service, but also because he had internalized a lesson on the meaning of "companionship" I had taught him at age fourteen on his first visit to Chalfonte. Mealtime had come and all were seating themselves at table. Ryan slipped into the living room. I followed him.

"Ryan, if it is uncomfortable for you to be present while everyone's eating, stay in here. But I want you to know you are welcome at the table. Your call." Without a word, Ryan rose from the chair and came to the table. Ever since, everyone at Chalfonte knows to set a place for him.

His thank you note after the Kensington affair included these sentences:

> Jimeyer, thank you for another wonderful weekend. I enjoy the time we spend together, no matter if it's the Canadian Rockies, or in Montreal, or in Toronto, or at Chalfonte House, or at my house. Because it's not the place you go, it's the people you go there with. And I must say I always meet some pretty cool people when I hang around with you. ... The Kensington thing was cool. It's a lot easier to work (and impress) such a small crowd. ... I hear that guest you had for the homily was pretty good as well. You should invite him to lunch or something....

Back to our train adventure years before. If any transient accommodation deserves the designation, "*If you have to ask the price of the rooms, you can't afford them,*" it is the Laurel Point Inn, Victoria, British Columbia. "Our reservations stated two beds", I insisted as we arrived by cab, travel-weary and hot off the ferry from Seattle. "I am very sorry, Sir," was the polite but firm reply. "All we have available is our ultra-luxurious studio suite with an extra long queen size bed."

I turned to sixteen-year-old Ryan as he was fading into the sunset. "Ry," I said, "I think I know you well enough to say that you are very secure in your (heterosexual) manhood. So am I. What do you think?" Ry nodded assent. My journal entry for that day reveals: The alternative was the parking lot. We took the room with harbor view -- and what a view it was! Quite possibly the most scenic hotel view I've ever had (same with Scammer) - a pond with an island, waterfall, scenic condos surrounding the small harbor and the sailing boats in the marinas!

It was while I was enjoying a Sapphire Martini and Pacific Rim Thermidor on the veranda, that Scammer shared with me that the smell of seafood made him nauseous. Only one solution --- he stayed at the far end of the veranda covering his nose while I leisurely savored my dinner."

I am bemused in reading my next morning's account of the prior night.

> Then came bed time last night -- 10 p.m. -- Scammer still on the Internet talking to Tim (Burgess), Chad (his older brother) and Karen (Tim's mom). Jimeyer is asleep on the bathroom side of the bed in about thirty seconds. Don't know what time Scammer jumped in --- all I know is that about 4 a.m. I was awakened by the sound of a trumpeting male elephant, who seemed to be right next to me. He was. Not wanting to stir his anger and retaliation, I tried various tactics to insulate myself from the uproar. Best solution seems to be stuffing my ears with cotton from the pill container and piling pillows between us and around my head --- plus visualizing myself having paid for and enjoying an African safari.

Even though I don't snore, (smile) not to be outdone in mammalian analogies, when we shared a hotel room in Montreal on a subsequent occasion, Ryan recorded the following: "Yes, even having to listen to the Blue whale in heat throughout the night was kind of funny."

Years later, Ryan records in his e-mail to Devin. "But our friendship has done nothing but grow from that first day I met him. I even went on a train trip with him across Canada in 1998 which totally rocked."

Though we visited some of the unique attractions in Victoria like Butchart Gardens, the greatest thrill for Ryan was discovering they had a school named South Park. A TV program with the same name entices early-adolescent boys. Ryan had donned one of his treasured tee shirts graced with a cartoon character from the show. He insisted we find the school so I could take photos of him at the entrance to brag to his friends back home. I didn't know what South Park was about, but Ryan, Tim, and Piecey had cautioned me that I was not old enough to watch it, so I didn't. Another reason I didn't watch it was that the Comedy Central channel on which it aired was not included in my basic cable package. Once it was and I saw a few episodes, I agree that my kids were right. I wasn't old enough to watch it.

Perched on the pinnacle of my pious priestly pulpit I perceive South Park as a parade of primitive, perverted, pernicious, pint-sized punks. "Potty-mouthed" is an understatement. Profanities, cursing, swearing and vulgarities spew from the mouths and bodies of these "innocent" fourth-graders as readily as sludge flushing down the toilet of a family with intestinal flu. Adding injury to insult, precious little Kenny is killed in every episode. The good thing is that the show does not air until 10 p.m. when I am ready for bed. The bad thing is that the show airs at 10 p.m. when the kids are ready to watch. Supposedly, there is a moral lesson in every episode.

We cancelled a planned train trip north to Courtney and back to Nanaimo, deciding to take a later coach/ ferry to the city of Vancouver, because Ry was experiencing gastric distress. I couldn't resist. "I think it's something you ate," I pronounced.

Vancouver is sometimes referred to as *Lotusland* because of its manifest Asian population, which began with an influx of people from south China over a century ago.

Perhaps his volatile gut impacted his disposition, but Ryan copped an attitude from the moment we entered the city. "I came to see Canadians," he groused. "If I wanted foreigners I would have ordered Chinese!" This persisted through a series of less than stellar encounters throughout our stay there.

Maybe it is my own obstreperousness, but I took silent delight in his attitude. I knew it didn't stem from prejudice; more from being taken by surprise. Middle kids, like Ryan and me, don't like surprises. We want to know what's coming. We like being in charge. My satisfaction came from knowing that our relationship was so genuine that he felt he could be himself. He didn't have to perform or attempt to please me, his mentor.

Typical of Ry's wry humor, within days of our return to Detroit I received the following postcard mailed from Vancouver: "I thought I was supposed to be going to Vancouver, not India! I'm just kidding ... I have nothing against these people.... I just feel out of place here... Wish you were here. Scammer."

All was far from negative in that beautiful vibrant city. Quoting from my journal:

>Lot's of rest Monday night, then yesterday, my "surprise" for Scammer -- a tour of the west coast repair and maintenance operation of VIA Rail, arranged through Kristina Sirsley, vice president of marketing in Montreal. Starting at 9 a.m., the entire morning and into

the afternoon is spent with Ali' Macaraeg, manager of marketing development, and Eero Kiutunen, chief of maintenance operations. My greatest thrill was watching Scammer drive the train, newly arrived from Montreal, to the automatic train wash, under the supervision of Engineer Charlie. Tee shirts and tokens are showered upon us --- as well as an invitation to a birthday barbecue on the platform....

Continuing the journal account ...
We are two blocks from Robson Street, which is in downtown Vancouver. People dress in extremes --- from jogging attire to "the nines". I fix lunch and finish laundry; Scammer writes cards. Then comes 5 p.m.. Scammer wants to swim at Pacific Palisades, across the street. I want to watch the first game of the Stanley Cup finals. (Scammer says hockey is boring.) We do both plus a red-hot ping-pong match at poolside. Evening is the Internet, pinochle and bed about midnight, after Scammer received his first Jimeyer massage and back-rub.

Throughout the years I have been doing massages, I counsel the kids to dress in bedtime attire, because when I am finished they will be so relaxed they will be ready for sleep. Often I have had to carry them to bed afterwards. True to form, Ryan remained fast asleep until 11:30 a.m. the next morning, his best rest of the trip. During the silent morning hours, I am content to keep vigil.

Those who have not lived with "special needs" persons are oblivious to the time and effort required of them to function each day, let alone feel well. For example, while in Vancouver we needed to call Sterling Heights, Michigan, to get a prescription filled. We had to go to several stores to procure Ensure (under a different trade name) --- with fiber

... not easy to locate in China. And we had to cart this stuff
around, sapping Ry's depleted energy and robbing us of
touring time.

At last, the climax of the trip -- the Gold Leaf service of the
Rocky Mountaineer Railway Tours. If you win the lottery,
or have rich friends to whom you can suck up, I
recommend it. Once on board the train, I needed to resolve
some glitches. Privately, I had made the staff aware of Ry's
eating habits, including his tube-feeding. With utmost
courtesy, we were asked if we wanted to dine at our seats
rather than with the other guests.

"Not on your life," I insisted, "reservations in the dining
car, please", knowing Ryan loves "eating out". We entered
to discover, they had cordoned off a two-person booth at
the end of the car. "Not on your life," I responded. Before
the marvelous trip was over, all the personnel realized and
were relieved, that we were to be treated "normally."

Jim and Margaret were our table companions. From several
points of view they were ill equipped to deal with Ry and
me. They were elderly, genteel, gracious and Australian.
We embarked upon our regular restaurant routine, complete
with its warped American humor. "I don't eat Mexican,"
Ryan announced as he dawdled with the ice in his water
glass.

A controlled but concerned expression crossed the faces of
our new friends as they surveyed the menu: "Poached
Alaskan Salmon," "Pasta Alfredo," "Quiche Lorraine".
You could read behind their faces. Mexican? Mexican?
"There might be other things you could eat, dear,"
Margaret suggested.

We delighted in the escalation of her mothering instincts in solicitation for Ryan's nourishment and welfare. Eventually I allayed their discomfort so they could enjoy their meals. "Ryan is the typical teenager," I proclaimed with authority. "You know how they are --- he has been eating --- all night long." Ryan smiled.

At Kamloops, courtesy of Engineer Bob Lewis and Rich Magill and their boss, Doug, Ryan was allowed to back the train into a switching yard. He unlinked nine cars. I trust all of the nine were bound for Jasper with another locomotive. It was a pity Ry was so exhausted. Try as he might, he couldn't appreciate the thrill to the fullest.

Next destination: Calgary and the Palliser Hotel. Upon debarking, the Rocky Mountaineer's staff presented Ryan with a magnificent train book signed with comments. Grateful heart in Ryan. Misty eyes in Jimeyer.

Our final leg is from Calgary to Minneapolis -- then on to Detroit. I get hassled in customs for having neither birth certificate nor passport. Ry slips by unscathed after review of my ownership papers of him. The flight is overbooked and Northwest Airlines is offering $1,400 apiece in travel vouchers to be bumped! Dollars dancing in his eyes, Ryan is whisked out of his lethargy. I offer to accommodate them if they would book us on a direct flight to Windsor on Canadian Airlines, a route I know is non-existent.

Meanwhile, I turn to Ryan for our final scam. "Look forlorn," I whisper. Ry obliges. "I realize you are overbooked in coach," I plead in my saccharine voice. "Would you be so kind as to book me and this young waif in first class?" She looks at me, then Ry, then me, then him. Expressionless, after clacking her computer keys for several moments, she hands me two revised tickets. We board the plane. After closing the hatch, the flight attendant announces they needed none of those persons who had agreed to be bumped. Ry and I "high five" each other --- from our first class seats.

Chapter 12: The Train Trip Postscript

Prior to our departure on his first big adventure far from
home and hearth, Cindy hovered over Ryan with motherly
admonitions, ending with "and take lots of pictures of you,
Jimeyer and the interesting places you visit." I scored big
time points with mom on this trip. I had taken photos of
Ryan and me. His pictures were of trains, tracks, trestles
and tunnels.

Life lies open and inexhaustible for most American middle
class young people. Returning from an elegant vacation
they can't wait to start new adventures with a "what have
you done for me lately?" attitude. Not so Ryan who
savored every morsel of our trip as evidenced on his
website (the_scammer.tripod.com). His humor and
creativity are reflected in an e-mail he sent me while
constructing the site.

> Jimeyer, Ok, so here I am looking through all the stuff
> from our trip. When I get to all the receipts and baggage
> tags, I say to myself, 'Self, it would be a good idea to
> laminate these things with the new laminater (sic) that I
> got for Christmas, so that they are protected and do not
> get ruined. It would also make it easier to scan on the
> computer so I can put them on my web page.' Then I
> say 'Self, that IS a very good idea. Go ahead and do it.'

> So here I am, getting the laminater ready, feeling all big
> and bad because I thought of a cool idea (This happens
> more than once a day) and everything is going fine.
> After I get all the baggage tags laminated, looking
> great, I start on the receipts. First the Ferry ride from
> Victoria to Vancouver. Yup, I'm cool. So I put in the

receipt and when it comes out the other side, I find that THE RECEIPT TURNED TOTALLY BLACK! At this point, I am in total confusion as to why that happened. (This does not happen often.)

Now, after that happened, I look at the airplane receipt. And I think 'OK, this one is on a different kind of paper, so it won't turn black.' So here I am, thinking 'Oh well, that was just a ferry ride. I didn't even get any pictures from that ride, so no big deal. But the airplane ticket I need, because it shows that I got to ride 'premium class' instead of coach, which I never did before.' In goes the pretty ticket stub. And to my amazement, IT COMES OUT TOTALLY BLACK, except for the 'Northwest Airlines' logo.

Why did this have to happen to me?!?!?!? The Scammer™ got Scammed?? That is totally UNHEARD of!! And all I can say is that it is all YOUR FAULT for not telling me that would happen. :- Scammed Scammer™

In the August after Ry and I had returned from our rail adventure, we were at Chalfonte House. He had alerted me "he had something special just for me." Then apart from the others, he led me into my room, closed the door, sat down next to me on the bed and played a cassette tape he had made. Only one song --- and the label on the case read: "To Jimeyer, from The Scammer, with love."

I had never heard the song before nor did I recognize either the artist or "10,000 Maniacs" with whom she had performed as lead singer. For all I knew Natalie Merchant was the name of a shop that sold spiffy women's apparel. After a few "na-na-na-na nas," the refrain continues:

You've been so kind and generous, I don't know how you keep on giving. For your kindness, I'm in debt to you, for your selflessness, my admiration. For everything you've done, you know I'm bound --- I'm bound to thank you for it." ... Oh, I want to thank you for so many gifts you gave, with love and tenderness... the love and the honesty, that you gave me, I want to thank you, show my gratitude, my love and my respect for you....

I lost it --- and locked him in my tearful embrace for several minutes; this sixteen year old kid.

Ryan later quipped to Devin: "I made him a tape of Natalie Merchant's ***Kind and Generous*** (know that one?) and that really moved him. It seems like we've known each other like since forever sometimes."

Ryan had a way, on this occasion and several others, of extracting my heart, expanding its capacity a hundredfold while insinuating himself inside, and then gently replacing it back into my body.

Relationships intensify in voyages of vulnerability far more than through adventures of joy. More than once in his life, Ryan has welcomed me as companion when he was being swept to the precipice of the fires of Hades. Returning to Detroit from Chalfonte after Ry presented me with this precious tape recording, I wrote the following in a letter to a friend.

Ryan thought that he might have picked up an infection from swimming in Lake St. Clair on Sunday, August 9, 1998... the usual stomach pains, the high fevers, and the shortness of breath. Admission to Children's Hospital of Michigan followed on August 14 as the high fevers persisted. Isolation because they had cultured gram negative pseudomonas. They cultured the blackened fluid that oozed from his G-J tube --- oxygen --- and of course, antibiotics. The scans showed pockets of fluid in the pleura, almost completely compressing the right lung. Dr. Klien had suggested a thoracotomy (again!) and decortication. Ryan, 'the Scammer' is NOT a good candidate for general anesthesia. Hopefully, our prayers are answered and that invasive procedures can be avoided, as he is responding to the antibiotic. Indeed, he may be discharged tomorrow (August 22) on home IV therapy...

This therapy was successful and no further interventions were required.

Chapter 13: Internet Connection

The previous sentence is not entirely accurate. "Further intervention" was required during this hospitalization, but it was "*a horse with a different collar.*" I sat beside Ryan as he struggled to organize his thoughts while emerging from days of fever and unconsciousness. "How's Tim?" he whispered. Not, "What happened to me?" or "I'm miserable" or "I'm scared." "How's Tim?" whom he knew in his stupor had been hospitalized at nearby Hutzel for insertion of another internal prosthesis in the leg that had had the cancer. Recovery from a prior surgery had not gone well and Tim's wound kept draining.

"Your patient needs to use his lap-top to contact his friend who also is hospitalized", I pleaded at the nursing station on 5 SW at Children's Hospital. "He needs to have his phone line activated so he can call out. Could you arrange that, please?" "It can't be done" was the curt reply.

I knew the answer was at best an evasion, at worst, a lie. Memories flooded back to when I was staff and/or volunteer chaplain in the decade of the seventies. I was the "only (chaplaincy) game in town" at Children's from 5 p.m. to 10 p.m. after I finished my work at Hutzel.

In collaboration with nursing, I fought for seven years to have telephones, which had been omitted intentionally from patient rooms when the new Children's Hospital building opened in February 1971. I recall the day of our "victory" in getting the phones. When I arrived that afternoon, the head nurse greeted me with, "Jim, the kids now have phones in their rooms." I did the proverbial leap of joy. "Not so fast," she added, "you are not going to be pleased.

75

The kids can't call out".

"Can't ... CAN'T CALL OUT!" I exclaimed as I dashed from the floor to the President's office. "YOU BASTARDS!" I raged at him. "You GIVE with one hand, and TAKE BACK with the other!" I could get away with these rantings because the President and I were friends, albeit at arm's length. He respected my ministry. "Not my decision," was his excuse. After half an hour of discussion, I left dissatisfied. Over twenty years later, the kids still could not directly call out.

"I know it can be done", I persisted with the 5 SW staff person, "it's a matter of turning a switch somewhere." Thus began a weekend of determination and fun for me: distress and anxiety for Children's Hospital staff. It was to my advantage that many remembered me from decades before; also to my disadvantage because many knew I would not be dissuaded from my "cause" whatever it might be. Many names here have been altered ---- to protect <u>me</u>.

Knowing no one was available from chaplaincy management, "I want to talk to the Patient Representative", I asked Monica. "We don't have one", she flipped back. Having had considerable experience with the requirements of accreditation review in my position at Hutzel, I was in her face with," Don't give that answer to anyone – Children's can lose its license for not having a patient representative."

From Gertrude I got another, "It can't be done" with the offer to call a hospital engineer to validate her reply. "Call him", I responded. Forty-five minutes later, two engineering-looking persons arrive to talk to me. "What kind of engineers are you?", I queried. "Heating and cooling", they replied. Back to Gertrude: "Don't – do –

that – to –me - ever- again", I snarled.

My juices percolating, I told Ryan I would return in half-an-hour. "Fifty feet of phone line, duct tape and a splitter, please," I requested of the salesperson at the Radio Shack store on Woodward Avenue. Then back to the hospital as if I knew what I were doing. The following production unfolded like an off-Broadway play. Observers' affects evolved from disdain, to curiosity, to acceptance, to applause --- all within hours. Ryan relished the performance.

"Need something?" the unit secretary inquired as I zoned in on the "doctor's telephone" behind the nursing station console. That phone was the only one with an outside line. It was separate from the communications operations of the floor. "No, I'm just going to attach this phone line and run it over to a patient's room", I announced with authority. "Oh", said the clerk and resumed her business.

"My god, you can't do that", nurse preceptor, Mary, screamed as I was duct-taping the telephone line to the hallway floor. "Would it be better if I went over the ceiling?" I replied, "Oh, oh, of course, not on the floor, not on the floor", she murmured as she scurried away. Just the "permission" I need, I said to myself, my legal mind churning. If challenged for threading the line through the ceiling tiles, my answer would be, "Mary, the nurse preceptor told me it would be better to do it that way."

I attempted to solicit the services of long-time friend, Jon Renaud. Adolescent boys loved Jon because he was a man's man and great nurse amid a sea of female caregivers. "Don't try to get me involved in your conspiracy," Jon retorted. "I know your game". He was right, of course. So I held the chair while comely nurse, Barbara, on her first day of work, laced the phone wire through the hallway ceiling tiles.

"I know you, Fr. Meyer", Julie, the acting head nurse shouted as she charged in horror toward the erupted ceiling, dangling wires and me. "You stop at nothing to get your way." I assured her that all would be tidy when we finished. A covey of medical students passed by. They thought my plan to hook up Ry's computer through the phone line from the nursing station was "way too cool."

As if I knew what I were doing, I attached the splitter at the telephone and had Ry connect to the Internet. Success! - and applause from curious onlookers. "Pick up the phone," Jon offered, knowing what would happen. Ry was disconnected. Only one way to remedy the situation. By this time I had the staff eating out of my hand. I took the phone from the nursing station, ensconced it on Ryan's tray table and ordered that if anyone wanted to use the phone they could check with Ry to determine whether or not he was on the Net. "Oh, okay", they assented. If our roles were reversed, I wouldn't have agreed with me.

Sunday night sweet slumber climaxed my weekend adventures. I suspected that the whole thing would be dismantled Monday morning when the more seasoned staff came on board. I fell asleep, organizing my intended lecture to the (new) President concerning phones and patient rights.

The telephone jangle aroused me from Monday morning dreams. "Jimeyer", Ryan's hoarse voice called into my ear. I interrupted: "Did they dismantle our telephone connection?" "Yes" he answered. My tirade continued for several minutes until Ry was able to curtail it. "Jim, Jim --- stop and think about it. I CALLED YOU. I now have an outside phone connection at my bedside."

At the hospital, chastened and head-bowed, I submitted to a reprimand from the head nurse. "I told you, Fr. Meyer, I would have the issue resolved if you would have given me time to do so...", she scolded. She added a lot more. I was paying scant attention. The legal principle of "precedent" was flashing neon in my brain. As we were taught in our college logic course, which was conducted in Latin, "contra factum non valet elatio" (*"one cannot argue against a fact"*). In other words, because it was done, it could be done. Henceforth no parent or child at Children's Hospital that I would be made aware of would be deprived of access to an outside phone line.

Whether due to Ryan's notoriety or mine, or both, upon readmission ten months later, Monique, the nursing supervisor was eager to inform us that she had made arrangements for Ryan to use his laptop from his bed. We smiled and thanked her for the courtesy. As of 2003, I understand all patients have equal access. Thank you, Jesus!

Chapter 14: Sexual Gratification

Was Ryan sexually gratifying to me? You bet he was --- if one believes as I do that sexuality is integral to being fully human and a complete man. Procreative? Indeed, as intercourse is understood as life giving. When penetration is to the heart, anything less seems inadequate and lackluster. What is the transitory thrust of a six and one-half inch probe when compared to the penetration of heart and soul? Which is more enduring and mutually satisfying?

Regretfully the language of genital sex co-opts the language of love, as in the term "lovemaking." My position is that this begs the question. True lovemaking is achieved in a total union of human beings, finding expression in legitimate physical contact, but going far beyond it. I do not denigrate physical sexual expression pure and simple. It is the wonder-filled and God-given desire and experience of most of humankind. My humble suggestion is that one ought to broaden one's view. Ought not all authentic lovers, celibate or not, challenge the premise that equates the language of love with the actions of lust?

I have facilitated grieving subsequent to the death of hundreds of children. Not uncommon is the candid confession of a dad: "I could more easily accept the death of my wife than my daughter", or of a mother, "… my husband rather than my son". Granting that lineage and genetics are reasons for these admissions, could it also be that the parent is affirming that being a child of her heart is more profound than being a child of her loins?

What of the child that was adopted at birth and raised throughout his lifetime in a loving home?

Ryan at the beach

Dare one claim that these parents are incapable of the depth of love of the father who conceived him or the mother who birthed and perhaps abandoned him? Given the breadth and depth of my relationships with children over years, I bristle when people proffer that I could never begin to understand what it is to raise or lose a child because I am a celibate priest.

Part of the genius of the love between Ryan and me was that it was mutual and respectful in every sense of the words. We understood that each was giver and recipient. I did not give or do more for him than he for me. If anything, the reverse is true. In this reciprocity, neither of us felt we had to tiptoe through the relationship. We were open and candid in our sharing, warts and all.

Ryan writes to Devin a few months before his death. ....
> I thought that this (Jimeyer) is a real cool guy to know. During the past five years, he has earned my utmost respect, he's a great friend, and I can honestly say that if it wasn't (sic) for him, and me meeting the people I did, I wouldn't have any kind of life.

These words in a private email to a close friend are hardly the language of a boy abused.

Unwittingly in his sentence above, Ryan expresses the lesson at the core of the Catholic Christian belief he practiced. St. Paul's Hymn on Charity, (I Corinthians, 13: 1-13), is well known because it is the text read at one hundred ten percent of Christian marriage ceremonies. However, in pursuit of the cool crescendo, *"there are three things that last, faith, hope and love; and the greatest of these is love"* (vs.13), the opening words are glossed over. The, *"If (I am) without love, I am nothing at all."* (vs. 2) Jerome Murphy O'Conner, O.P., a preeminent scripture scholar, provides pertinent commentary:

> Love, more accurately, 'loving,' is the very being of the
> Christian. And for Paul there was no difference
> between being an authentic human and an authentic
> Christian. The two were interchangeable. Verse two,
> 'without love I am nothing,' is not a statement about
> utility, it is a statement about existence. Without love, I
> do not exist!

Does not this statement parallel Ryan's words?

Murphy-O'Conner continues:

> <u>What makes A</u> (read Ryan) *alive, is this loving*
> *relationship with B* (read Jimeyer).
> Similarly B to A; or B to C.
> <u>You cannot love in the abstract. You must love another</u>
> <u>person. It must have a human object so that **the very**</u>
> <u>**being of A is constituted by this relationship to**</u>
> <u>**B**</u>.(emphasis added)[4].

[4] Cited from Fr. Jack Castelot, S.S., Scripture Lectures, St. John's
Center, Plymouth, MI, on June 20, 2002

I Loved a Boy

Chapter 15: The World of Investing

How to introduce this eager sixteen-year-old to the world of investing? "*Learn by doing*," they say, so I concocted a plan whereby Ry would not only experience the vagaries of our capitalist system, he also would learn about "socially responsible" mutual funds. Knowing a minor cannot enter a binding contract; nonetheless I prepared the following document on my legal letterhead stationary:

To all those who shall read these letters, be advised:

On the seventeenth day of the ninth month in the year of Our Lord, nineteen and ninety-eight, the undersigned parties being of relatively sound mind, did enter and consummate the following agreement, to wit:

RYAN, 'THE SCAMMER' GIANNINI...shall have a five hundred dollar ($500.00) pecuniary interest in the Domini Social Equity Fund (DSEFX) a mutual account owned by the REV. JAMES L. MEYER, aka: 'JIMEYER.'

No actual money shall be exchanged nor shall any fees be assessed at any time. Scammer's interest is as follows: He alone shall determine the date of disposing of his interest, but not beyond September 17, 2003. Within ten days of the date of disposition, he shall pay to Jimeyer monies or legal tender (excluding pennies) equivalent to any loss in the value of the stock from the values indicate in the subsequent paragraph. Correspondingly, Jimeyer agrees to pay to the Scammer within the same ten days, any increase in the value of the stock.

84

At the close of trading in the New York Stock Exchange on the aforesaid day, shares in the aforesaid Fund were trading at NAV of 28.02, hence MR. SCAMMER'S interest would be 17.8444 shares.

In the event Jimeyer shall dispossess himself of the aforesaid stocks, he shall make compensation to the Scammer at not less than the prevailing prime rate, calculated on the principal amount listed above, (np. $500), compounded on an annual basis...

Ryan monitored the course of his "investment" on a daily basis, sending me e-mails of adulation for Mr. Greenspan, chairman of the Federal Reserve Board, whom he came to refer to as "Alan." He chose to liquidate after holding his investment for eleven months. Regretfully he did not follow the tried and true investing principles I practice "religiously" (pardon), namely, *Buy high. Sell low.*" I had to write him a profit check for $133.00.

Regarding Ryan's longevity, I confess applicability of the adage: "*I couldn't see the forest for the trees.*" That I should have known better from my thirty years' association with sick and dying persons, hospitals and medicine is irrelevant because it is rational. My relationship with Ryan was not rational. I could not, I would not, I did not countenance in others, or myself the possibility that Ryan would ever die --- until I was blindsided on August 22, 2002.

Chapter 16: Alarms Sound

Mortality and morbidity alarms sounded once again, in the summer of 1999, when Ryan was sixteen and a half. I cancelled a study program at Notre Dame University to be at his side. My following four e-mail messages, his reply and my postscript tell the story:

First

Please be advised that Ryan (The Scammer) Giannini was taken to Children's Hospital by ambulance late this morning (Thursday, June 17, 1999), where Alexa Canady, MD, Chief of Neurosurgery, immediately operated to remove hydrocephalic pressure from his head. It was also determined that he has bacterial meningitis. At this hour, I will be returning to the hospital to be with him and his family in the ICU. If things continue to go well, he should respond to antibiotic therapy and in about a week, a permanent shunt will be placed in his head. It is likely that he also will have a permanent tracheostomy[5]. Please lift him up in your thoughts and prayers....

Second

Late this morning (Saturday, June 19, 1999) Ryan had a central line inserted so he can receive TPN (total parenteral nutrition). A line was also placed in his wrist (to obviate multiple blood draws). Two issues are prominent: rampant bacterial meningitis (which well could have occurred through an infected sinus) and (relatedly), his cerebral pressure keeps elevating. I failed to mention at the outset, he has been intubated

---

[5] A tracheostomy is an incision in the windpipe to allow passage of air and removal of secretions. Henceforth Ryan's breathing would be through a tube in his neck rather than through his nose and mouth.

(placed on a respirator) since the procedure on Thursday. Good news is, he has been alert and appropriately responsive since the surgery. Again, please lift him in thoughts and prayers....

Third

This afternoon, Tuesday, June 22, 1999, Ryan the Scammer Giannini was extubated (his breathing tube was removed)! Also, though he's still in ICU at Children's Hospital, the infection seems to be under control. Now, we are waiting to see if his head will absorb the excess fluid. He's not feeling great, but feeling BETTER THAN HE WAS. Lots of questions yet need to be answered ..but we rejoice! THANK YOU, JESUS....

Fourth

It felt SO GOOD sitting with an alert and bright-eyed Ryan, playing backgammon and two handed pinochle (and winning 14 units!) yesterday afternoon, Friday, June 25, 1999. As most of you know, Scammer holds a very special place in Jimeyer's hierarchy of loved Chalfonte Kids. Earlier in the day, the drain in his head (which had been clamped off for two days to see if he could absorb the fluid without resorting to a shunt) was pulled and the hole sutured. Head and stomach aches that had plagued him from the beginning have subsided significantly, antibiotics have eliminated the infection; the only pain med he requested yesterday was an AM Tylenol. He is on his regular tube feedings, up and about, even able to take a bath. Consults to Neurosurgery, ENT and GI have yet to be evaluated. Praise God and thank you for lifting him up in your thoughts and prayers... it has meant A LOT to him. Special thanks to his friends for the cards and those who have e-mailed him through me.

Ryan's reply: Friday, July 2, 1999
> Get-Well-Wishers: Thank you so much for
> thinking/praying about me over these past two weeks I
> have spent at Children's hospital. They definitely were
> not the greatest two weeks of my life (except for the
> Demerol and morphine :-)) (smiley face) but I
> managed to get through it, just like all the other times.
> And I think one big reason was from all the well wishes
> and prayers from all of you. I enjoyed reading your e-
> mails that you sent Jimeyer to send to me. Just knowing
> that people were wishing me well made me feel great.
> Now I am trying to get back in the swing of things back
> home, and hopefully, I'll be back to 'normal' (I use the
> term loosely) in no time. Ryan The Scammer™

Jimeyer's July 14, 1999 postscript: "He's still being
evaluated (five hours in hospitals on Monday, July 12) - but
HOME and doing so much better TG! Love, Jimeyer"

Ryan returned home without tube, shunt or tracheostomy.
One month later he was at Chalfonte with his friends. He
records in the guest book what that meant to him:

> Our plan worked out perfectly. Tim would fake that he
> was having surgery on Monday so that we could get a
> few extra days up here.... I enjoyed seeing Big Bink,
> Scott, Cheri and the Bakers - they are an inspiration to
> all of us campers. 16 & 17 (year olds') week ruled big
> time. The trio of Tim, Jon and I just cannot be beat. The
> addition of some female types were pretty cool too
> (even though 3 of 4 were Timlins). Evin has to be the
> toughest kid, because he really took some verbal
> assaults from everyone ... Counselor Rachel had us
> doing all this 'ultimate' stuff which never resulted in a
> winner except for me and my wet-t-shirt; YES!

...massages were pretty much the theme this week, as well as talking like Jimeyer, DANG!

WARNING: DO NOT RENT THE MOVIE 'As Good As It Gets.' It's horrible! Pointless! (I bought it and tried to convince the kids it was great) I tried to show everyone what some good watchings were, but the Village Market didn't' have any South Park episodes. Figures. So we rented 'Bean.'.. These past 10 days were absolutly awesome. Seeing everyone having fun, and playing euchre for money is all one needs to enjoy life. 'Making Memories' (as Emily would say) happens everyday at Chalfonte house, and I am truly grateful to be a part of these memories. Thank you for inviting me up again, and hope (smile) I'll be back soon. I love this place and everyone who comes up here. Love, Ryan, 'The Scammer' Giannini

Chapter 17: Empowering Spirits

Behind the first line of Ryan's entry above is a story of touch and of empowering spirits. As the priest, I would like to claim initiating the plan to lay hands on Tim prior to his surgery. I can't. It was the unchurched Rachel Timlin who suggested, planned and directed it. As I share what we did and how we felt, I recommend that you plug in your own stories of similar phenomena. We all have them, though too often we dismiss them as "coincidences."

This is the background. Tim Burgess was diagnosed with osteosarcoma at age eleven. I had ministered to him and his family during several hospitalizations, starting when he turned twelve.

Karen, his mom, reminisces.
> In February of 1995 we almost lost him to pneumonia. He was running a high temp and the pneumonia was so bad it didn't show up on the x-ray. His white count was about four. For three days they watched him around the clock 'til he finally showed signs of improvement on about day five.

Tim has been a "Chalfonte Kid" ever since. In the summer of 1999, he was sixteen, facing the possibility of the amputation of his right leg above the knee.

Memories of Craig Richards were not far from us. A close friend to Tim, Craig was a Chalfonte Kid with osteosarcoma, having had a similar amputation at about his same age. Craig's cancer metastasized (spread) --- and he died at age seventeen on November 8, 1998. In Tim's case, two issues were paramount: one - that the cancer had not spread and two - that amputation, though

"Laying on of hands"
Rachel Timlin, Rebekah Timlin-Meddles, Jon Piercey, Tim
Burgess, Ryan Giannini

probably inevitable, could be delayed as long as possible until Tim grew more. Earlier that week a terrified Tim had come and gone from Chalfonte for the impending surgery. We wished him well. He returned the next day because his surgery had been canceled. This time the laying on of hands occurred prior to his departure.

Rachel recalls:

We gathered in the living room after dinner, not really knowing what would happen. No one needed an explanation of why we were there - that was perfectly obvious. We lit a candle. I remember it being hard for anyone to form words significant enough for such an occasion. So, in true Chalfonte style, we all just said what we felt.

"We'll really miss your leg, Tim". "It's been a great leg". "Do you mind if we call you Stumpy when it's done?" "I can carve you a wooden peg if you want." We all stopped talking. Jimeyer said a few words, and Tim's body felt lighter under my hands. We talked about love and healing, and the amazing strength we gained simply from being in each other's presence. We directed our love to Tim, and he felt lighter still. I can still feel the connection we made - through, around and with Tim - it was love, it was strength, it was light and it was HEALING.

"C'mon people now, shine on your brother" played on the stereo. (*"**Get Together**,"* popularized in the sixties by the Youngbloods.) Between Tim's Eminem and Jimeyer's anti-Vietnam records, this song seemed most appropriate. There was silence as we sat together - still and calm... then, in true Chalfonte style, we all just said what we felt. "You're unstoppable, Tim." "We've got you back." "We love you, Tim." "We love you...."

I recall I took a position where I could rest my hand on his right leg, the one that had had the cancer. I felt radiating power in the silence of our intertwined spirits. When the service was over, I was certain the cancer had not spread and that amputation would not take place on this occasion.

In listening to these kids tell of the event, understand that we are not talking about a gathering of the church choir. These were real normal teens. For example, a staff member described Jon Piercey ("Piecey") in the guest book as: "The biggest pervert of them all." After his experience, Jon had this to say:

> …So we all gathered, lights were turned down. I'm sure some prayers were said by Jimeyer and then the music started and so did the laying of the hands. It was totally silent other than the song in the background. Everyone had a hand on Tim. I had mine on his leg that was giving him trouble and for the length of the song everyone sat in prayer for Tim. For me it was more than prayer. It was a deep meditation that brought me closer to Tim than I've ever been. In the meditation I felt me, Tim, God and all the others around. But it was focused on me, Tim and God mainly. The others were just there for us it seemed, which was really comforting.
>
> The song was probably only a few minutes long but for me it seemed like an hour of pure peacefulness; peacefulness I've never felt before. I felt fully and completely sure things would be fine the next day in surgery. Besides the unbelievable oneness I felt with Tim, I really felt fully complete. This came from the positive energy of everyone around us that made me truly feel a oneness that I've never felt since. It was a feeling that only was there for actually a few minutes but a feeling that I won't ever be able to forget….

Tim remembers all the details, especially the striking coincidence as the doors to surgery swung open.

Due to some very bad timing I was slated to have surgery right at the beginning of my week at Chalfonte House. What this meant was two days up north with my friends, and then a week in a hospital bed, not a very good ratio. The first couple days came and went very quickly. Now it was time for the three and one-half hour ride home, a short night's sleep and an early drive down to Detroit. Everyone said goodbye and wished me luck. Nothing out of the ordinary.

I arrived at the hospital early the next morning, feeling a little bit nervous. I was going in to have an operation that could vary between, making my leg better, or taking my leg off. I had been in multiple other surgeries before by this time, so I wasn't too shocked when the doctor was running a little bit late….Six hours later it was a different story though. I had been lying there, in my gown, hooked up to IVs all morning, and into the afternoon. This isn't what I left my friends up north for. I had my parents go find my doctor for me so I could inform him that I would not be having surgery on that day. I was gonna go back up north.

The fact that in the last three days I had driven for about twelve hours didn't really bother me; I made it back. The week came and went quickly, as it always does, only this time the goodbye was a little different. The idea had come from a Chalfonte veteran, Rachel Timlin. We all joined together in the living room of the Chalfonte house. I was lying on the floor, and all of my friends were in a circle around me. Everyone placed their hands on me while the song ***Get Together*** by the Youngbloods played in the background. Although the song was only about four minutes long I could have swore we'd been doing this for hours. I could physically feel the love of all of my friends. After that I was ready for anything.

That is not the end of the story though. While I was waiting, for the second time, to go into surgery the song *Get Together* by the Youngbloods came on over the hospital's radio. Just as I was sitting there amazed that this was happening, a nurse walked back and told me it was time to go in. As they finished prepping me and wheeled me back, I listened to the entire song, with it just ending as I was getting on the operating table.

After the laying on of hands, Karen and John, Tim's parents, remarked to everyone about the striking darkness-to-light contrast in Tim's attitude from his aborted surgery earlier in the week and his return for what resulted in a "corrective" surgery.

Four months later, in what is described in medical parlance as "an uneventful procedure", Tim had the amputation. Ryan picked out the perfect get well card to bring to his companion at the hospital on the day he had his leg removed. Always the considerate one, Ryan wanted to do his part to assist Tim in his recovery.

"I heard you are not feeling well," read the front of the card. And inside, "I hope you will be back on your **feet** soon." (emphasis added) Ryan had crossed out "feet" and underneath inscribed, "foot." On Tim's birthday, Ryan presented him with --- a jump rope.

Chapter 18: The Best and the Brightest

Ryan's mom feigned being miffed at him when he was listed among "The Best and the Brightest Italian American Students" in the August 1999, **Italian American** (newspaper). Under his picture were the words: "Most influential persons: Fr. James Meyer and Mr. Gene Collins (teacher)." "All the others had their mother named along with a teacher," she chided. "But you named Jimeyer"! Ryan shrugged. I held him close.

Ry e-mailed,
> Jimeyer if you're not doing anything for lunch at 11 a.m. on Thursday, September 16, 1999, you might meander over to Neiman Marcus in the Somerset Collection (a mall), there's a thingy going on and I'm getting an award.

This was about as close as Ry ever came to requesting a "command performance." Here was a kid that made demands on no one. I discovered this "thingy" was a "biggy." It was entitled "Beat the Odds Scholarship Award Presentations" hosted by a prominent local newsman, Mort Crim, along with Michelle Engler, First Lady of Michigan. Ryan received a one thousand dollar college scholarship plus a new computer, one of seven finalists of the two hundred entrants.

His essay, Beating the Odds, reflects not only his personal philosophy, but also his public persona:
> Some people think that when the odds are against them, they should cash in their chips and call it quits. While this is a perfectly fine way of thinking, some people see it as a challenge and push harder, to get the odds back in their favor. Well I am one of those people who push back, back at life, and try to beat the odds.

Ryan Giannini and Jimeyer at the Awards Banquet
Ryan's essay, "Beat the Odds" won the prize

The odds that I am overcoming is my so-called "disability". I have Gorham's syndrome, which basically is a deterioration of the bone. It has slowly progressed since I was about seven years old, from my teeth, to my jaw, and to the spine in the back of my neck. Without my teeth or jaw, it became hard for me to eat solid food, so I had to have a feeding tube put in to get my nutrients and maintain a healthy weight. And with the spine in the back of my neck deteriorating, I had to have a rod put in place of the bone in my neck. There were also many visits to the hospital, some three months long, but I will leave them out because I will run over my one page limit if I include them.

Because of my illness, and frequent visits to the hospital for treatment, I was put on home schooling in the sixth grade. The home-school teacher only came to my house twice a week, for one hour each visit. Now anyone knows that you can't learn a whole lot in two hours a week, so I was left to pretty much teach myself the schoolwork. This went on for about four years. By the time high school rolled around (tenth grade) I was feeling pretty good. I decided to give a few classes a shot, but still keep the home-school teacher in case I couldn't keep up. Besides the usual nervousness any kid would have entering high school, I had a few other worries: How would the other kids treat me? Will I be able to keep up with five days a week? Will I get good grades?

And to my surprise, trying out those two classes was a very positive experience for me. I made a few friends, had good grades, and even had a little fun too. Now here I am in eleventh grade, taking five classes, maintaining a 3.8 GPA, and looking forward to attending college.

If there was one thing I like about my illness, it is that I get to meet a lot of caring people, people who want to help me out. And that makes me feel good.

So I have decided to help others out, and make them feel good too. I have joined the Students Offering Services (SOS) club at my school. The SOS club, among other things, holds fund-raisers for the ill, helps the handicapped, and visits nursing homes. I also help out the Michigan Humane Society by taking animals into my house that would otherwise be put to sleep because of illness. I get to care for dogs, cats, puppies and kittens until they are healthy and strong enough to be put up for adoption.

There are many choices that need to be made over the course of a lifetime -- some big, and some small. And the way in which we choose to deal with them can say a whole lot about that person. As for me, I may back down from some situations, but not without giving it my best shot first. Because no matter what cards life throws at me, I will come out a winner, and beat the odds.

In seeking my private counsel the week following his award, Ryan lifted the veil just a mite to reveal his true feelings and concerns.

Jimeyer, OK ...here's the deal: I want to have surgery after I get out of high school to 'fix' me up. This will probably require many surgeries, which will take a long time. My mom says that since I have these scholarships that I should go to college and then have the surgeries. While I can see her reasoning, I don't like that idea. If I were to go to college before the surgeries, I would have pretty much no social life, and stay away from people not saying anything to anyone.

I know now that it is hard for people to understand me when I talk, and it makes me frustrated sometimes when that happens. I don't want to have to do that at college, because talking to other people, especially strangers who you don't even know, is something that you almost HAVE to do when you're away like that.

My disease has been pretty much 'gone' for the past few years, although there have been complications from what has been done. And I have been waiting to get 'fixed up' every since the summer of '96 when I was supposed to start reconstruction, but got a pleural effusion instead. (However, if it wasn't for that incident, I never would have met you ☺ (smiley face).

It's not that I can't accept what I have, but I know things can be different. Before all this happened, I was a very outgoing person, and I said whatever was on my mind. Now I only talk when something absolutly (sic) needs to be said. And because of that, I am not involved in any groups at school, and I stay away from places where there are alot of people and noise because I know that if I did, I would just stay in a corner or something and not get involved. I WANT to get involved. I don't want to be like that if I don't have to, or if there is a way to change that. I'd like to know your opinion on the subject. Ryan

Graduating in June 2000, Ryan had decided to remain living at home while attending Macomb County Community College in the fall. He planned to transfer to Walsh (Business) College in two years to complete work on his MBA. I treasure his thank you note at the time of his graduation.

Jimeyer, thank you for coming to my graduation party. I'm glad you could make it (being the busy person you are) and I hope you enjoyed yourself. Thanks also for the perfect card and for the good wishes.

I also want to thank you for introducing me to the physical and spiritual place that is Chalfonte house. I honestly don't know where I would be if I never met you, and all the friends from Chalfonte House and E.R. (Elk Rapids). (They brought me a nice amount of $$ at my party too :-)). (smiley face) [6]"I am honored that you would pick me to help carry on that Experience. After knowing you for about four years, it seems like we've known each other forever. I am very thankful for that. OK enough of that mushy stuff--- I don't know where that came from! Thanks again, Love, Ryan The Scammer.

The summer of his graduation, we consulted various experts to address Ryan's concerns and improve his circumstances. One was a speech pathologist who suggested Ry use a small microphone all the time. He tried it at home in front of us. Understanding him was vastly

---

[6] I selected Ryan to be one of three permanent directors of the **Chalfonte Foundation**, a separate entity from Chalfonte House. The Chalfonte Foundation is a 501 c. 3 (non-profit, tax-exempt public foundation – EIN#38-3568149, at www.chalfonte.org) whose mission is: "To provide spiritual, psychosocial, recreational, financial and educational support for children, youth and other individuals and families in need.... locally and around the world." I established it to carry on the work after my demise.

I chose Ry because I like him and it doesn't cost anything to take him to lunch, but more so because, like me, he is cheap. Preservation of assets is paramount with me. Profits made from the sale of this book will go to the Chalfonte Foundation to further its mission with the likes of the kids recorded herein.

improved. He would have none of the microphone. Though unstated, I am certain he felt it would be one more thing that made him "different."

Ryan compensated for his voicelessness in his prowess for instigating contention. Like dangling wigglers in front of trout, Ryan baited the kids of Chalfonte that summer by suggesting that some of the older kids forsake their designated vacation week to be relegated to the younger kids' week.

There was a flurry of serious responses to his e-mail, sent to kids and staff alike. Under the heading: Uneven Distribution Chalfonte House, he concludes:

> Don't get me wrong, I don't have anything against these people or anything. If there was actually room for these people ... I would be more than happy to have them up. Because they are nice people. So please consider these 'improvements' to the 'bunkie list'! It would make life easier for us in the long run. After all, I am just looking out for the people who are going up. Because I'm a considerate person.

Ryan confides to me:

> Don't you LOVE all the commotion that my one little e-mail created? :-) (smiley face) It's funny how everyone is taking it so seriously. I've gotten e-mail from like everyone saying how they would sleep on the floor or something if it bothers me so much. I RULE!

Chapter 19: College Commences

In the fall of 2000 then into the winter and spring of 2001, Ryan immersed himself in his college coursework. But as if to remind himself and the rest us to keep our priorities straight, he forwarded the following poem he picked up on the Internet entitled ***Slow Dance***. His terse notation: "nifty poem."

Refrain:
You'd better slow down. Don't dance so fast
Time is short. The music won't last.
Have you ever watched kids on a merry-go-round?
Or listened to the rain slapping on the ground?
Ever followed a butterfly's erratic flight?
Or gazed at the sun into the fading night?
(Refrain)
Do you run through each day on the fly?
When you ask "how are you?" do you hear their reply?
When the day is done, do you lie in your bed
With the next hundred chores running through your head?
(Refrain)
Ever told your child, "we'll do it tomorrow?"
And in your haste, not see his sorrow?
Ever lost touch, let a good friendship die
Cause you never had time to call and say 'Hi'?
(Refrain).
When you run so fast to get somewhere
You miss half the fun of getting there.
When you worry and hurry through your day,
It's like an unopened gift thrown away.
Life is not a race. Do take it slower.
Hear the music before the song is over."

From the time Ryan sent it, I have not adverted to the poem
*"**Slow Dance**"* until assembling my notes and transcribing
it on February 12, 2003. Ryan had sent it to me two and a
third years earlier on October 20, 2000. On February 13,
2003, the poem was forwarded to me in an e-mail from
someone I did not know. I opened it because the sender's
address looked familiar. I do not open e-mails from
unrecognized senders. Coincidence in the timing?

The tale gets more delicious. Purportedly, it was written by
a young girl with cancer who had only six months to live
and forwarded by a medical doctor from the Bronx. A
message appended states in part: …

> PLEASE FORWARD TO HELP THIS LITTLE
> GIRL. By you sending this to as many people as
> possible, you can give her and her family a little
> hope, because with every name that this is sent to
> (name of a recognized organization) they will
> donate three cents per name to her treatment and
> recovery plan.... PLEASE PASS THIS ON AS A
> LAST REQUEST

I did not pass it on. Real or scam? I don't know. But right
now Ryan the Scammer is looking over my shoulder --- and
smiling.

Chapter 20: More Alarms

Like every loving parent when I got up at night, I would walk through the bedrooms of the Chalfonte kids. I would survey my kingdom with satisfaction, smiling at the children in slumber. I abandoned the practice as adolescents passed into adulthood. Big mistake on Sunday, May 27, 2001. Ryan was eighteen. It was 8:30 or 9 a.m. when I thought to check on him.

"I'm sick," he whispered as I entered his room. He didn't need to tell me. He looked awful. "Could you please go to the store and get me a decongestant?" We explored options from the decongestant to driving home. I was ever fearful of his need for intubation (insertion of a breathing tube). The anatomy of his mouth and throat were so compromised that only a supremely skilled physician could position the tube with dispatch.

Temperature taken -- 103 degrees. We agreed upon Munson Hospital in Traverse City, thirty minutes away. Ryan was so weak he hardly could move. With Jon sitting beside him in the back seat, we sped out of town. "Sped" is the correct term. The cop and I agreed, sixty-five miles per hour in a twenty-five mile zone is not kosher, even on a sleepy Sunday morning in Elk Rapids, Michigan. I could have been shot as I jumped from my car when the patrol car pulled me over. The officer must have read the determination in my eyes as I glared through his windshield, hands held high.

"I've got a very sick kid in the car, and you can either help me or get out of the way NOW," I commanded. Much to my surprise, he did as I demanded.

"Don't speed," he felt compelled to shout back. "Yes, officer," I replied, under my breath more like, "YEAH, RIGHT!" Subsequently, I thanked the patrolman to his face and commended him to his chief.

Five days in the hospital with another pneumonia in his right lung, he cultured positive for Pastuerella Multocida. The doctors shook their collective heads because this organism is associated with the saliva from farm animals. Not once this weekend did I see Ryan kissing a cow.

Later, he wrote,
> Jimeyer, Geez this is getting old. I'm starting to feel like you with all these thank you cards! But I guess it's worth it, especially for you 'taking care' of me last weekend. I would have much rather stayed at the house than have that happen. Even with the hot nurses, the narcotics and the insurance money, I like being with friends better. :-) Thanks. I'll try to be better and not do this again. Love, Ryan.

Danger of dying? Not on my watch, not in my mind; no --- never. Within two weeks of discharge, Ryan was in Beaumont Hospital with aspiration pneumonia.

In July, he sent a Q & A profile from the Internet to many of his friends. I've excerpted a few of his answers that give insight as to how he lived and how he felt. The preface to the e-mail was: "Okay...normally I don't do these, but I'm really bored right now. Sorry. But who knows...maybe you'll find something out about me that you didn't know. - Ryan"

Q. Which day of the week is your favorite?
A. Monday (RAW) (Wrestling), Thursday (SmackDown!) and Sunday if there's Pay-Per view.

Q. When did you last cry?
A. I honestly can't remember.

Q. If you were making a movie about yourself, who would play you?
A. Definitely Robin Williams.

Q. What is the #1 goal in your life?
A. To make other people happy.

Q. If you were another person, would you be friends WITH you?
A. Heck yeah! I rule!

Q. Do you follow or lead?
A. I am my own person... I do what I want, when I want, how I want. If it means leading or following, it don't matter.

Q. Who is your most trusted friend?
A. Jimeyer.

Q. Who gives the best advice?
A. Scott B. (Scott Brinkman)

Q. Do looks matter?
A. It depends on what I'm looking at. :-} (smirk)

Q. What are you addicted to?
A. This stupid computer.

Q. What do you do to vent anger?
A. Listen to music.

Q. Who is your second family?
A. The Chalfonte gang.

Q. Do you trust others easily?
A. Not really.

Q. Who makes you feel loved most?
A. My family.

Q. Have you intentionally hurt another person?
A. Of course.

Q. Do you like sarcasm?
A. Absolutly(sic)! Life is not complete without it.

Q. Do you feel understood most of the time?
A. Haha. No.

Q. Have you thought seriously about committing suicide?
A. Yes.

Q. Are you a vegetarian?
A. I guess you could say I am.

Q. Do you think you are strong emotionally?
A. Very.

Q. Best news you've heard lately?
A. Things are progressing nicely for something I've been
   waiting years to happen.

Q. Do you care about the way you look?
A. If I go out somewhere, then yes. Otherwise, no.

Q. When you don't know the answer in class, how do you
   bail yourself out?
A. Haha! When I don't know the answer. That's a good
   one!

Q. Which of your friends has the easiest phone number?
A. I don't know. I don't use the phone, so I never ask for phone numbers.

Q. Have you ever been stalked?
A. If I was, the person did a pretty good job.

Q. What teacher can't you stand?
A. The ones who can't teach.

Q. What's your favorite quote?
A. "You can do anything you want, as long as you follow the 'three I's': Intensity, Integrity, and Intelligence." (Kurt Angle, Ryan's favorite wrestler.)

Ryan's "Yes" in answer to the question: "Have you thought seriously about committing suicide?" at once ripped into my gut and comforted me. I yearned to press him to my heart and never let him go to protect him from all harm. I am consoled that Chalfonte gave him friends and solace. After his death, when broaching his answer to the suicide question with Cindy, his mom, she sighed and whispered, "his answer doesn't surprise me".

Chapter 21: Chalfonte Memories

Pity-partying is not part of Ryan's profile. I recall the tenderness of heart I felt one evening in August of 2000 when he excused himself from the dinner table. Okay for him because he couldn't eat. He reappeared from the upstairs kitchen -- with homemade brownies for dessert. Now it's August 2001 and he approached all of us with a form to sign under two columns and no other notations. "Boys" - "Girls" were the headings. As I added my signature to the others, I mused, "What a nice thing he is planning; perhaps a home-made greeting card or something else special."

The paper reappeared on the frig, this time with the heading: "All those who have affixed their signatures below have agreed to participate in the wet tee shirt contest." Though all were "consenting adults," this crossed my line of acceptability. The previous steam-shower party with boys in trunks and girls in bikinis was okay, but this was too much.

"Ryan, are you serious about this?" I queried as I took him aside. I knew I would not get a straight answer. He stood in front of me with his characteristic smirk. I was trapped -- or so he thought. As quoted earlier in the book, youth and skill are no match for old age and treachery.

I attached the following words to his paper: "It is agreed. All those who have signed below WILL participate in the wet-tee shirt contest; the boys as contestants, the girls as judges. (signed) The Management." Soon after, two words appeared appended to mine. "Management Sux." The contest was aborted.

Fun and food at Chalfonte
Jimeyer with Michael Hunt, staff member

I Loved a Boy

We must maintain our Chalfonte dignity. Another rule is that the "f _ _ _" word may never be used. Chalfonte kids refer to it as "dropping the F-bomb". I did not fall off a Christmas tree. I am aware that after my usual 10:30 p.m. retirement, the "F-bomb" may have exploded once or twice over the years.

Someone had sent me an amusing and clever e-mail. I concocted a scheme whereby Piecey, Tim and Ryan would read it before the group. Recognizing the thin line between humor and mockery, I felt compelled to solicit Ry's prior consent. Notwithstanding his garbled speech, actually, because of it, I wanted him to read the "tongue-twister" parts. All three were enthusiastic about participating in the scam and studied their scripts.

Feigning anger, I accused them at a breakfast gathering. "Piecey, Tim and Ryan! I understand that last night you dropped the 'F-bomb' many times over. Be prepared to give a report tonight." To the unsuspecting crowd after supper that evening, they presented: *Historical Roots of 'The Finger' Gesture*:

Tim: "In the current film, **Titanic**, the character Rose is shown giving the finger to her fiancé's manservant. Many people who have seen the film question whether 'giving the finger' was started during the time of the Titanic disaster, or if it is of more recent origin, perhaps invented by some defiant seventh-grader."

Piecey: "According to in-depth research at a major university, here is the true etymology of the gesture."

Tim: "Before the Battle of Agincourt in 1415, the French, anticipating victory over the English, proposed cutting off the middle finger of the captured English soldiers. Without the middle finger, it would be impossible for the archers to draw the string on the renowned English longbow. Therefore, they would be incapable of fighting in the future."

Piecey: "This famous weapon was made of the native English yew tree. The act of drawing the longbow was known as..."

Ryan: "'plucking the yew' or 'pluck yew.'"

Tim: "Much to the bewilderment of the French the English won the battle in a major upset. They began mocking and taunting by waving their middle fingers at the defeated French, shouting..."

Ryan: "'See, we can still pluck yew! PLUCK YEW!'"

Piecey: "Over the years some folk etymologies have grown up around this symbolic gesture. Since pluck yew is rather difficult to say, like..."

Ryan: "Pleasant mother pheasant plucker."

Tim: .."which is where you had to go for the feathers used on the arrows for the longbow, the difficult consonant cluster at the beginning has gradually changed to the labiodental fricative 'F.'"

Piecey: "Thus, the words often used in conjunction with the one-finger-salute are mistakenly thought to have something to do with an intimate encounter."

Tim: "It is also because the pheasant feathers have traditionally been used on the arrows of the longbows, that the symbolic gesture is known as..."

Ryan: "giving or flipping the bird."

Piecey: "And yew (y-e-w), all thought yew knew
     everything."

I will control my impulse to name her, but it was a year
later before at least one in the audience learned it was a put
on.

The following is a portion of Ryan's longest entry into the
Guest Book, written on August 18, 2001:
> Jimeyer, this week was absolutly (sic) awesome. Stuff
> happened that probably shouldn't have, and stuff that
> probably should have happened didn't. I don't know
> how it is possible, but every year seems to be a little
> better than the last. Seeing the old faces again (interpret
> that as you wish), and sharing time with this awesome
> group really is something to cherish and hold on to.
> Where else can you get to spend such quality time,
> having fun, being yourself, hanging with friends? It's
> amazing to me how our group gels so well with each
> other.
>
> Maybe it's fate, or maybe it was planned all along.
> Whatever the case, I feel I am blessed to be a part of it,
> and to be a part of everyone's lives. Right now, I'm in
> the Geriatric Living room, all alone, as everyone has
> taken off for home, well except for Paul, but come on –
> I can only take so much of him. Alright, enough deep
> thinking from me. Now on to the good stuff....
>
> The week started off with me, Piecey, Margaret,
> Burgess and (after a slight detour), Evin getting a ride
> up to ER in a sweet RV, complete with oven, sink, 26"
> TV, VCR, microwave, bedroom and bathroom. I'm
> thinking that the Chalfonte Foundation should invest in

114

one of those.

It is just wrong to name a dog "Mary." "Mary" is a person's name. Not a dog's name. Even for a Timlin, that's pretty bad.

A digression here. All week Ryan had been merciless in badgering Erin Arbogast and Daniel Timlin about naming their dog, "Mary." One more example of Ryan's delectable humor is the following account told me by his mother after his death.

> Here's the story about Mary. On May 30, 1989, when Ryan was seven years old, he had his first surgery. The nurse who I asked to be in the room with him was Mary Jo. In pre-op she gave him a stuffed Old English sheepdog. We decided to name her Mary, after Mary Jo. Ryan brought Mary with him to many other surgeries as well. ... somewhere down the line, mom noticed Mary was becoming a little dirty so she washed her and also put her in the dryer. Needless to say, Mary did not look like herself after that, and Ryan was quite upset with me. Ryan didn't take her with him ... April 28, 1993 because he was getting a little too old to be seen with her, as he was eleven now.

He never let on to this history; he savored it in solitude, like sipping a thirty-year old Madeira alone before a quiet fire on a cold winter's night. Ryan continues his account of the August, 2001 week:

> Watching meteors was pretty cool. Sunday service was very good, especially since I picked out the music. Our Canadian friends ...introduced two awesome new games, Rummy-o and Maffia/Gangster. Naturally, I am good at both, but I think I'm better at Maffia, cuz it runs in the family. People were staying up until some crazy

times. Even Jimeyer was up until 3 a.m. a few nights. Daang. What is this world coming to? This low water stuff is really sucky. You gotta walk out about five hundred feet just to get water past your knees (slight exaggeration).

But it was all good, especially with the wave runner… we all went to Sleeping Bear[7]. The smart ones stayed on top of the four hundred and fifty foot drop (myself included), and those who don't have all the shingles on their roof went down.

Cards sucked all week for me. I think I lost about ten dollars. But that's because I was playing against Mara. What a cheater. It kept her happy, so that made it worth it. It was fun trying to cram eighteen people and two dogs in the van, just so we wouldn't have to pay for four vehicles at Sleeping Bear.

This year, instead of Chef's Assistants we had Chef's Ass. I have to say, they did have some nice ones too. The Sportsmen's Club was a blast as usual (Ha ha, get it, blast!) Jimeyer actually picked up a nine millimeter and hit the target. Kind of makes me wonder if he has done that before.

Me, Burgess, and Piecey were forced to do some research on a certain F-bomb, due to frequent usage along with its corresponding hand gesture. I can now say that the labiodental fricative will have a whole new meaning for me and everyone else. The word needs to be spread about those pleasant mother pheasant pluckers! Whole – bathroom steam shower parties rule!

---

[7] Sleeping Bear Dunes National Lakeshore Park is located on the pinkie of the mitt that is Michigan's lower peninsula.

For the most part, this week had no structure whatsoever. But I guess trying to get twenty people to do the same thing isn't the easiest thing to do. I give tons of credit to the staff for doing everything they did. I don't think there is any other team that can work that kind of magic. The chemistry between them, and with the campers, is something you don't find everyday. That's what makes this place so great. Everyone who comes here is accepted, and becomes part of the group. Even if your name is Margaret.

It feels really 'empty' right now. Not only in the house, but also in me. After spending a week with a bunch of great people, then being alone in the house is definetly (sic) a whole different experience.

Chapter 22: Epitaphs

It is eerie that unbeknownst to either, both Ryan and Kenny Wallace said their goodbyes and wrote their epitaphs in the Chalfonte Guest Book the year before they died. In previous years, neither had written with the volume nor the intimacy as is recorded in these entries. Kenny was to die at age seventeen, seventeen days before returning to Chalfonte in 2000. Ryan died within the week after returning from Chalfonte in August 2002, but the brevity of his entry in that latter year witnessed to how sick he was.

I have mentioned Kenny earlier as the CFer with ADHD and Tourette's Syndrome. Due to his tiny stature and immature looks, he could substitute as a Christmas angel in the tableau at the local Baptist Sunday School. However, 'neath that cherubic facade, lurked a mind and mouth overflowing with adolescent lechery. When he would read aloud from the ***How to Repair Plumbing*** book, even I was having lustful thoughts. All of this aside from his incessant need for six liter flow of oxygen (very high level) and enough daily medications to fill a valise.

On August 7, 1999, Kenny wrote:
> Dear Jimeyer. I've had a really fun time here at Chalfonte house this week. I'm glad I got to meet these new teens! I enjoyed everything we did. I especially liked the guns cause now when my cousin and I argue about who's the bigger man, I can say I've shot the most powerful gun!

(Kenny blasted six clay pigeons in a row with a twelve-gage shotgun when Ed and Amy Greziak and friends hosted the kids at the Elk Rapids Sportsmen's Club.)

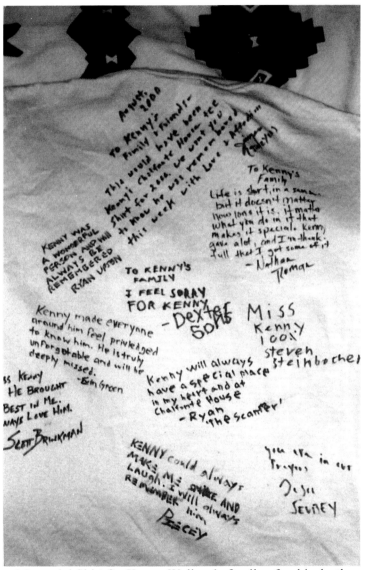

Memorial Shirt for Kenny Wallace's family after his death

But that's not all! The best reason I come back each year isn't cause of the chicks, food or adventures we go on. No, it's the people I love and meet. Why does time have to FLY when you're having fun with the people you love? Where does time go? And I learned the mystery of morning wood too! (smiley face). I will miss all the Chalfonte members very very much! I hate saying good bye! It's so HARD ON ME! There I said HARD ... ON! (bigger smiley face).

When I get home from Chalfonte house every year I cry for at least a week before I can realize I am not coming back till next year, so I can see the people I love. I don't know where in my life I would be if it wasn't for meeting Jimeyer! I don't think I'd even be alive. THANK YOU Jimeyer, I really appreciate you letting me come to your very lovely home this and every other week I've been here!

Then he concludes in capital letters:
PLEASE FIND IT IN YOUR HEART TO INVITE ME BACK TO CHALFONTE HOUSE NEXT YEAR. LOVE, KENNY WALLACE.

Ryan continues his epistle of August 2001, as if he is engaged in closure. The entries are unique in that he names every person and ends by saying to each, "I love you!" He writes:
And now, I'm going to run through everyone who was here and say a few things:

STAFF
Jimeyer – NONE of this could have happened without you. without your vision, without your love. I am honored to be a 'student' of yours, and I want to learn more. I love you!

Chalfonte Board and senior staff at Ryan Giannini Park (RGP)
Jon Piercey, Erin Arbogast, Daniel Timlin, Patti and Paul Hresko, Tim
Burgess, Blair Grammer, Scott Brinkman, Jimeyer and Cheri Giroux

The Chalfonte Gang
Back: Ryan Giannini, Ryan Upson, Andrew Johnston
Middle: Jimeyer, Emily Upson, Eddie Carter, Chad Giannini
Front: Amy Conover, Trevor Banka, Kelly Hresko, Jon Piercey

Scott – your reassurance, caring, humor, and knowledge have helped me in more ways than you could ever know. Thank you for being there. I love you!

Cheri – If Scott likes you, I guess you can't be all that bad. (Kidding – I should get a dope slap for that) your gentle, caring and concern for me and for others is something I admire. I love you!

JE & Ginny – the Canadians. I have never known a more cooler couple than you two. I don't think there is a single person you don't get along with. And you two are very free spirited with life. I love you both!

Paul – you haven't been around long, but you definetly have impacted everyone that walks into Chalfonte House. You are truely an angel. I love you!

CAMPERS
Burgess – one of my bestest friends in the whole world. It's always great spending time with you. Your humor and views of life are the best. I love you!

Piecey – another one of my bestest friends. Get a new computer, damn it! Thanks for being a friend, for taking crap from me, and giving it right back. I love you!

Evin 2.0 – the new version. I like this one. I wish you and Kay the best of luck, and maybe next year, you'll get to be a spoon. I love you!

Emcare – Those nights chatting on the computer really meant a lot to me. That you would be open with me like that is cool. Oh, and thanks for the $2. I love you!

Upchuck – We didn't do too good with euchre. But

that's mostly your fault. I love you!

Andy – I love it how when you say even the stupidest things, they sound funny. Just remember to ask yourself 'What time is it?' I love you!

Alisha – It was a pleasure to meet you. If anyone can keep Andy in line, you would definetly be the one. You fit in perfectly here – ROCK on! I love you!

Trevor – your determination never ceases to amaze me. Last year it was the 11 minute dune climb and this year the one-legged bowling. Keep that going and the best of luck to you. I love you!

Brooke – what can I say – you got the steam party going. And for that, I love you!

Blair – the local. It was great to meet you. Hopefully you can come back during the year so we can get to know you better. I love you!

Kelly – the blonde (crossed out) brunette (crossed out) blond. Your strength is amazing, and your love for life just shines through your smile. I love you!

Margaret – you have so much to offer this group – you do fit in, you just need to nudge in every now and then instead of sitting back. I love you!

Mara – Glad you could make it this year. Your singing is awesome, and so are your many other talents (palm reading, stacking the deck…) I love you!
Rebekah & Scott – you didn't stay long – that's not good. And Scott made Mexican food, so that isn't good either. You must make that up- I love you!

Dan – I think you need to go to dog naming school. Seriously, I met you the very first time I came up here, and for some reason you've been nice to me ever since. Thanks for just being you. I love you!

Erin – A person who has a love for animals just as much as me. And the fact that Jimeyer allows you to bring two dogs up here shows how you can get just about anything with those 'puppy dog eyes.' I love you!

Alright, I think that's it (phew!) If I forgot anyone, then you're probably not that important anyway."

Ryan ended his entry with this simple enigmatic reference: "***These are days, you'll remember***" *-10,000 Maniacs.*"

I have retrieved the lyrics of the song "**These are the days**" by 10,000 Maniacs:

> *These are the days*
> *These are days you'll remember*
> *Never before and never since, I promise*
> *Will the whole world be warm as this*
> *And as you feel it,*
> *You'll know it's true*
> *That you are blessed and lucky*
> *It's true that you*
> *Are touched by something*
> *That will grow and bloom in you*
>
> *These are days that you'll remember*
> *When May is rushing over you*
> *With desire to be part of the miracles*
> *You see in every hour*
> *You'll know it's true*

I Loved a Boy

That you are blessed and lucky
It's true that you are touched
By something that will grow and bloom in you

These are days
These are the days you might fill
With laughter until you break
These days you might feel
A shaft of light
Make its way across your face
And when you do
Then you'll know how it was meant to be
See the signs and know their meaning
It's true
Then you'll know how it was meant to be
Hear the signs and know they're speaking
To you, to you

Chapter 23: Innermost feelings

Because the heading was Discussion Sheet, therefore semipublic, I don't feel it inappropriate to reveal some of the concerns Ryan shared on a spiritual retreat with his church youth group in October of 2001.

Question: What are your three best qualities?
Answer: My humor, my faith and my attitude on life.

Question: Is there anything you do just to be different?
Answer: I will do <u>anything</u> to make people happy/smile.

Question: What are your three greatest fears?
Answer: The unknown, the future and not being all I was
  made to be.

His angst is not without foundation as he reveals in his answer to: "In what areas of your life are you struggling with? Explain."

Ryan writes:
  I have a big health 'thing' coming up in the near future, and it will affect my future greatly. I don't know how – no one knows how. And I'm not doing good with the opposite sex. I'm really starting to want to find someone to share my life with.

We are being propelled into 2002 and Ryan's fateful reconstructive surgery of February 12. Ry sought support from his faith, his family and his friends to allay his fears.

At a gathering at church, Ryan chose his pastor, Fr. John, (not his real name) to anoint him with the oil of the sick, laying hands upon his head, while praying the traditional words: "*Through this holy anointing, may the Lord in his love and mercy help you with the grace of the Holy Spirit. May the Lord who frees you from sin, save you and raise you up.*"

Desiring, dare I say, needing his friends present, who could resist his e-mail invitation with the heading: **"Ryan to get laid at high noon, Sunday, February 10. Please come."** After getting our attention, he writes: "To help prepare me for my journey there will be a 'Laying of the Hands' service for me. I would just like for you to be there…"

Once again, Ry conceals his feelings with humor. On February 6, he had written the following candid e-mail to his beloved brother, Chad. Therein he spells out the importance of the love of individual family members and friends to sustain him in life. The first time Chad chose to share a portion of this private memo was at Ryan's funeral.
  Chad ---
  So yeah, this isn't your 'normal' e-mail from me. I know we've talked a bit about my surgery and what not, but you're probably in the dark about a bunch of stuff. So I'll fill you in.

  You know I've been waiting a long time for this to start happening. It's been about five years since I was supposed to go in for reconstruction, and that got shelved because I ended up going in the hospital for three months over the summer. Even though that happened, I'm so glad it did, because if it didn't happen, I would not have met Jimeyer and more than half the friends I have now. And these are true friends, who will do anything if I need it and stand by me for whatever, so that was a good thing.

And now I'm at that same point, but now it looks more like the surgery is going to happen. And even though I don't show it, I'm scared as hell. I mean, I go to the doctor, and he tells me flat out "I don't know what's going to happen after the surgery." That's not the most comforting thing in the world. And this is from a world-renowned reconstruction doctor.

This is something I want to do though. I don't need the surgery so that I can live, it's not something that has to be done. It's something I want. Maybe I'm being greedy, I don't know.

And it's going to be a long battle, mostly uphill before it starts to level off. There will be more than one surgery, and I'm probably not going to look any better than I do now for awhile. Which really shouldn't matter, but it does in a way.

People always say they don't care what other people think, but that's a bunch of bull shit. You can only ignore it for so long. I don't show it, but it does bother me. I get that stare from people, people pointing, people calling me a girl or ma'am (especially the shoppers at work) and the most frustrating part is not being able to carry on a conversation unless it's dead quiet. And even then I have to repeat myself.

So I'm hoping that by going through these surgeries, those problems can be eliminated. But like I said, it's not going to happen with this one surgery. Heck, it might not happen at all. I could come out much worse than I am now. But I'm not going to plan on that. I'm not planning on anything really. I'm just going to live how I've lived my whole life. I will take whatever God gives me, and make the most of it. Because that's all you can do.

Some people would just shut themselves in from the rest of the world. But that's not good enough for me. I've been given this time on the earth, so I'm going to use my time to the fullest. Not a day goes by when I don't thank God for all that I have.

And the biggest gift that I have is my family and my friends. Their love and support, YOUR love and support, is what keeps me going. I could never go through this surgery without that. I'm doing it for myself, but in a way, I'm doing it for everyone else by showing that I can pull through. There's no big gain without a big risk.

It really means a lot to me knowing that you're with me all the way. I have always looked up to you my whole life, for the person you are. You do some of the things I can only dream of. Hopefully after this surgery, I will be on my way to making those dreams a little closer.

Yet, even if that doesn't happen, just knowing that you will still be there to support me means so much. If I didn't have that support, I don't think I could go through with this. It's a huge step for me. Up or down, wherever it may be, I know that when I come out I will have the same people standing by my side.

As for my feelings, I say screw the stairs. I'm taking the elevator. And --- I'm pushing the 'Up' button. Thanks for being there for me in the past, now, and in the future.

I love you,
        Ryan

Chapter 24: Reflections on the Chad Letter

Years ago, I had introduced Ryan to the peace movement. Convinced of its importance, he attended and absorbed the contents of several conferences. The following is a reflection on the meaning of his life in the context of current US foreign policy:

Ryan's premise can be summarized. "What sustains me in life --- is the love and support of individual, identifiable family members and friends." This truism confounds the anonymity beneath whose mask torture, humiliation, violence and destruction are pursued. We use terms like "terrorist," "enemy," "menace to the world" and "axis of evil" to depersonalize those upon whom we choose to apply the ugly works of war. We anesthetize ourselves to render invisible to mind and heart the trembling adolescent awaiting her school bus that will never come because the bridge has been destroyed.

Chris Hedges, who admits to being addicted to war as a foreign correspondent for fifteen years, says:

> Lurking beneath the surface of every society, including ours, is the passionate yearning for a nationalist cause that exalts us, the kind that war alone is able to deliver... We abandon individual responsibility for a shared, unquestioned communal enterprise, however morally dubious.[8]

---

[8] p. 45 "***WAR is a Force That Gives Us Meaning***" by Chris Hedges, 2002, Public Affairs: Perseus Books Group (used with permission)

The atrocity of war and violence can be understood when seen in the prism of an individual life. The paradigm for Ryan's story is Sadako and one thousand paper cranes. You may not recall the story, but you know the context. Less than three score years ago, seventy thousand persons were incinerated in less than a minute when the United States government dropped the atom bomb on Hiroshima, Japan. Soon after, more than twice that number died of radiation exposure.

Sadako was among the latter victims, dying at the age of twelve. While in her last agonies, she tried to fold the thousand paper cranes required to insure her wish for healing according to the legend. She died with three hundred forty-six remaining to be folded. She never gave up. Her classmates finished her mission.

Hedges goes on to say:
> A soldier who is able to see the humanity of the enemy makes a troubled and ineffective killer. To achieve corporate action, self-awareness and especially self-criticism must be obliterated. We must be transformed into agents of a divinely inspired will, as defined by the state, just as those we fight must be transformed into the personification of unmitigated evil. There is little room for individuality in war[9].

Ryan and Sadako's message is **life giving.** War is **life-taking.** It's as simple as that. They counterpose a national frenzy and fear wherein the arrogance of power dictates violence and destruction as the vehicles to life and love. Their legacies remain for us: to enfold the world in the remaining cranes of peace they were unable to complete.

---
[9] pp. 73-74 - ibid

131

Chad's private reply to Ryan's e-mail is no less telling:
Ryan,

Thanks for the e-mail. It really means a lot to me. I've always had a hard time verbally telling people how I feel, and it's always been better for me if I can write to them, so I want to let you know what's going through my mind and what I'm feeling.

I'm glad you wrote me and I know you are scared, and so am I. I guess I haven't really thought about the big picture here. For a while now it's just been, "Ryan's having his reconstructive surgery and everything will be fine." Well, as you know, that is a very limited and maybe even an ignorant statement, because this is going to be the biggest and greatest challenge of your life to date. I didn't realize that until talking to you and reading your e-mail.

I guess I was always in the dark about what going on with you and that is something I wish I would've spoken up and asked. Because every time I would tell someone about you they would ask me questions that I couldn't answer because I didn't know the answer. I guess that isn't as bad as not knowing how you feel inside. I know it is frustrating for you, and I can't even begin to imagine what you feel. I just took that for granted. I never really stopped to think what's going on in your head.

You are a very strong person, but even the strongest of people feel bad sometimes even though they don't show it. Yes, I do understand why you want this surgery done though and I'm 100% with you. No matter what happens like you said, it's going to be a long uphill battle. You are going to have good days, and you are

132

going to have horrible days. But one thing is that I believe in you and so does everyone else. You can do this. I only wish I had half the mental toughness you do.

You know, I remember the first day that this disease affected you. Dad and I went to K-Mart to fill a prescription for you because you were in so much pain. I also remember seeing you for the first time after you got your halo put on. I really didn't know what to think and what was going on. I knew that you had a hard time holding your head up and that the halo would help, but I didn't know how serious this was. I mean, I hear mom and dad talk to people now about the last few times you were in the hospital and they talk about how the doctors didn't know if you were going to live or die. I never knew that is what was going on.

But you are so right. I'm glad too that it did so you could and did meet Jimeyer and all your other friends. But through all of the complications, you didn't let that stop you. You could've easily given up. But you didn't. You have this spirit in you that does not quit. If you go back and think about everything that has happened with you, one of the things that sticks out most is the number of people you've touched. It's not countable. From all of our family and friends, to the nurses and doctors and the new people you've met that are now your friends, and the friends whom you don't really see anymore. You've had an effect on so many people.

I mean, nobody could ever count you out. When you were in the hospital, you opened up your own store. I know I always tried to scam food from you, but you just kept on beating the odds. You were one step ahead. But I'll tell you what, even though you don't know that, I want to tell you that you have affected me too. Shoot, even before that disease started, I remember when I had my brown beanbag and you had your blue beanbag, and we used to wrestle with them.

I remember you playing soccer, well you were really more interested with playing with the ants, but when the ball would come by you, you would jump first and then kick, which of course, you missed. You also loved playing with those spiders too. You would find some rolly pollies and put them on the different spiders' webs just to see how big each spider was. Then there was always going to see trains, and the one time when we had to, "quick, get off the track! Amtrak is coming!"

But through all those memories, what means the most to me is your support. You are right when you say that I support you 100% and I'll always be there for you. But I'm glad to know you are there for me too. Even though at this stage in your life you can't be physically involved with sports, I'm flattered and honored to know that you can and are mentally involved through me. Whether is its wrestling with little Tim and Chase, or playing basketball in the driveway or at the park, or even messing up that Willa dog with GORE!!

I love when you come and watch me do all those things because it means the world to me just to see you smile. I know you are dying inside to mess around with Chase and Tim, or Gore Willa, or even playing b-ball. But we both know it can't happen at this moment in time. Shoot, I love it when you come and watch me play b-ball at the park and mess up everyone there. You're my hero man. You've done and accomplished so much given so little. That's actually a funny statement because you have spirit, love and God in your life and that will take you far, not to mention the 3 I's.

I can't imagine my life without you in it. I have to tell you that I know there are a lot of possibilities with this surgery, and I've thought about all of them. I have to tell you that I've thought about the worst case, and like I said, I don't want to think about that but it pops up in my mind. We just have to keep on praying and let God take care of this. No matter if it happens in this lifetime, or in our afterlife, I will promise you that one day you will be able to run and jump and play and do whatever you want, and I'm going to be there right next to you. I can't wait for that day to come.

But I'm also going to be there for you in your hard time too. Especially recovering from this surgery. I will help you out in any way you need it. You're so many things to me. You're my hero, my inspiration, my friend and my brother. I'm just glad to be all those things because nobody else in the world can say they are all those things. I'm here for you, I'm pulling for you, I'm praying for you, and you will be fine no matter what happens. You will have a long road ahead of you, but you'll make it! I love you.

Your big brother, Chad.

Chapter 25: The Big Surgery

My emails begin to color in the picture of this momentous occasion.

Ry's Surgery, 2/13/02, 8:44 a.m.

Ry, 'the Scammer' Giannini approached surgery on Tuesday, February 12, 2002, with the utmost confidence after imposition of hands and the sacrament of the anointing last Sunday at St. *Polycarp Church, *(not the real St. Fish) surrounded by family and friends. He entered the operating suite at Providence Hospital promptly at 1 p.m.. It was not until 9:30 p.m. that he was wheeled from the recovery room to the ICU, fully vented, sedated and unconscious, his head sheathed in bandages. As had been anticipated, fiber optic ventilation proved impossible and so he was put fully on the breathing machine.

The world renowned Dr. Ian Jackson in collaboration with another plastic surgeon worked all day and were able to accomplish major reconstruction of Ry's face, nose, eye orbit floors, and upper jaw with a huge piece of bone removed from his left hip. As both commented however, due to the uncertainty of his disease (Gorham's Syndrome) only time will tell whether or not the reconstruction will remain intact or also dissolve. I was with Ryan and his parents all day yesterday and will be with them today as well. Please continue to lift all of us in your thoughts and prayers. Love, Jimeyer.

Ry Giannini Update 2/14/02

…Though breathing on his own and being aware all day yesterday, Wednesday, February 13, they have not removed the breathing tube from his throat. He communicates only by note. Add to that, his eyes are swollen shut and most of his face is enormously swollen as well. Without going into detail, Ryan's head pain has been excruciating for most of yesterday, to the degree that lesser men (including me) would have 'succumbed' to whatever. Many of you who receive this email can personally relate to the degree of his pain.

Though he experiences 'positioning discomfort' I don't think he is yet aware of the pain he will experience in his left hip where they had removed a huge portion of bone for reconstruction. His 'numbers' remain excellent, though there is some concern for congestion in his right lung (the one wherein he had a pleural effusion a couple of years back). There is talk of removing his breathing tube today, which will be done in surgery, due to the precariousness of his intubation. Please continue to pray for Ry, his family and me. Love, Jimeyer.

End of St. Valentine's Day Report 2/14/02 9:40 p.m. I may sleep well tonight. Having spent most of the day in the ICU at Providence Hospital, I can report that Ry spent a very restful day. His numbers including 0_2 sats remain excellent. Variously throughout the day, his pain was indicated at either 7 or 5. Most of the day he slept peacefully and recouperatively. Though he cannot as yet open his eyes, they have been tested and are focusing appropriately. The swelling in his face has reduced significantly. He has not complained at all about hip pain, tolerating positioning on his left side for a considerable time.

Hopefully, he will be extubated tomorrow morning when all of the 'right people' will be on hand to intervene if necessary. After extubation, nutrition may well commence, (good, but not very exciting for him --- 9 cans of vanilla Ensure). Your support is greatly appreciated. 'Hero' cards may be sent to his home at …(address) thank you, thank you, thank you. Love, Jimeyer.

In Ry's Own Words 2/23/02

Hey everyone, I'm at home now! I can't say that I'm doing 100% right now, but that dang hospital wanted to kick me out as soon as possible. (I have no clue why they would want to do that … especially someone like me). But I'll take the $675[10]..

I must say I was totally unprepared for what happened. Even with the whole 'I don't know' scenereo (sic), this was hard for me to take. I went into surgery on a great high – not just from the meds – but from the Laying of the Hands service just a few days before. That really put my mind at ease knowing I had the prayers and support of all those people, who would be there with me until the end.

So I get out of surgery – about five hours- and I'm hurting, as was expected. But what I did not expect, or anticipate, was the MAJOR swelling that happened as a

---

[10] Years before I had encouraged Ryan and his family to buy one of the insurance 'products' that pays $75 directly to the patient for each day of hospitalization

result. My face was about as big as a pregnant watermelon. Literally. I was still intubated (had breathing tube in my mouth) so I couldn't talk. My eyes were swollen shut. And the throbbing in my head made it almost impossible to hear. The hours went on like days.

I kept wondering if this was worth it? In the back of my mind I knew the answer, but the pain was so much that it took over. Wednesday, Thursday, and Friday came around, and not much difference. My mom and dad would tell me that the swelling went down allot, but it wasn't enough for me, because I still couldn't see. For those three days, I was communicating by writing stuff down on a pad of paper (that I couldn't see) and hoping that my writing was legable (sic). I was pretty lucky, because I had the same nurse for those days, and she got to know my needs pretty good. (I heard that she was also pretty hot too… but I couldn't see that. &*^$)

Friday they took the tube out of my mouth, which was no walk in the park. After having it in so long, you build up lots of drainage in your lungs, not to mention that you have to learn to breathe on your own again. That wasn't fun. That night, because now I was breathing through my mouth, my nose got dried up, so I could only breath through my mouth. Which in turn made my mouth dry. So I couldn't sleep. (Motrin only puts you to sleep for so long)

Things started to stabilize, so they moved me out of the ICU on to a step-down unit. I still couldn't see. Saturday, Sunday, and Monday were spent just sitting up on bed, listening to stuff. It's funny how I took it for granted waking up every morning being able to see. Not any more. It sucks. So I had my mom read some books to me, the newspaper, and had her bring in a boom box that she would set up. At this point, I wanted to have visitors so bad, but I would want to see the people when they came in. That's why I put out the 'no visitor' thing. Maybe that was being greedy on my part, I don't know.

Anyway, Monday night, I was able to open my right eye a little bit. That made me so happy. Until I tried to go to sleep. My right eye was now open, however it wouldn't shut. So that kinda sucked. Tuesday my Left (sic) eye opened, which was good. And I had full use of the eyelashes on that eye, so I could open and shut it. That led to me getting a patch over my Right (sic) eye, to prevent any dust or whatever from getting in my eye. And that's exactly what's going on now. I'm typing this e-mail with one eye. And my vision isn't all back to normal yet either. Things are still a bit blurry.

I got home today and the first thing I wanted to do was to open up the cards that everyone had sent. I didn't open them sooner cuz I couldn't see (remember?) I think I had about 50 of them. That made me happy. Especially the home-made ones. Those were my fav. But like I said before, just knowing that I have all those people behind me – all of you behind me – really means a lot.

So yeah, I'm home now. I'm still in some pain, but it's tolerable. It's gonna be a few more days or even weeks before things get back to 'normal' again. But I'm ready for 'em :-} (smirk) Thanks for your prayers and support, and I'll be writing more later – Ryan.

Thank God for Ryan's times of boredom, like March 6, 2002. He would create and dispatch his answers to surveys.

I Loved a Boy

Therein he would lift the veil to reveal his private thoughts. His replies occasion a spectrum of emotions in me.

Q. If you could build your house anywhere, where would it be?
A. It'd be in Elk Rapids, MI. (home of Chalfonte House)

Q. What's your favorite article of clothing?
A. I've got this nice blue shirt that really brings out my eyes… drives the ladies wild.

Q. Where's our favorite place to be?
A. Anywhere with friends.

Q. What's your favorite TV Show(s)?
A. WWF, Pistons, South Park, Who's Line, Screen Savers.

Q. What's your favorite childhood memory?
A. Just being a child, doing all the things that I can't do now.

Q. Favorite restaurant/café/eatery?
A. Do I have to answer this one?

Q. Do you believe in afterlife?
A. Yes.

Q. What is your least favorite household chore?
A. I don't do household chores. That's women's work. (I'm gonna hear it for that one) :-} (smirk)

Q. If you could have one superpower, what would it be?
A. Read people's minds. Although I'm pretty good at that now.

Q. Who was your first love and at what age?

A. Umm… I don't remember what her name was, but I was in second grade, and she was our class 'Safety' during lunch and recess. (So I started early).

Q. Use two words to describe yourself?

A. Funny, sincere.

Q. Do you prefer the city & crowds or the country & quiet?

A. Country and quiet, cuz then you get to think without distraction and get to see the beauty of the earth. But I still have the option of going into the city every now and then.

Q. What are you most grateful for in your life?

A. The people that I know.

Q. If you were to pass away at this moment, do you know where you are going?

A. Probably to a morgue.

Twelve days later, on March 18, I sent out the following terse email:

> Please continue to lift up Ry in your thoughts and prayers. For more than a week, he has been experiencing constant severe intractable pain in his chest. Physicians have ruled out heart and lungs and suggested it is 'muscular skeletal.' It does not appear to be related to his surgery. Love, Jimeyer.

I wouldn't admit it in my note, but I dreaded the reemergence of his Gorham's Disease which could ravage his facial reconstruction. Next day he was admitted to Troy Beaumont because of the pain. He spent the next two weeks on IV antibiotics to treat severe infection and pneumonia in his right lung.

Wedged between his hospitalizations and his pain, Ry and I were able to spend April 13-18 in Florida. Ry was comfortable enough to be dropped off at Ft. Myers beach for several hours each day. When I picked him up, he would sigh and quip to me: "Jimeyer, please make it during spring break next year. At this time, the scenery sucks!"

As usual, I received a card from Ryan on my May 6 birthday. The gold and cream lettering on the front declared: "100 Years Young." Inside he penned:

> Jimeyer, sorry, this is the closest I could find to your actual age. Happy Birthday and many more! Don't plan on turning in anytime soon, cuz I still have a lot more to learn. With Love and Admiration, Ry Clops.

And his entry in the Chalfonte guest book for Memorial Weekend said in part:

> Jimeyer had to leave early for a funeral (dang people going and dying) so we were left alone Sunday afternoon/night and Monday. It sucked because there should never be Chalfonte House without Jimeyer....

Chapter 26: Josh Sheldon

Josh Sheldon was a twenty-four year old CFer listed for a double lung transplant at the University of Wisconsin at Madison. On July 11 he had a massive pulmonary bleed and was not expected to live.

The living and dying of Josh are important hues to complete the portrait of the summer of 2002. Josh and Ryan were symbiotic both in the magnitude of their suffering and in the manner they celebrated their lives. They had abiding concern for each other. I recall one August morning after returning to Chalfonte from Josh's bedside in Detroit late the night before. After his usual sleepless hours kneeling on the floor with head propped up against the edge of the couch because he could not breath laying flat, Ryan queried: "How's Josh?" Upon my response, he shook his head and whispered: "I could never go through what he is going through!"

And after I read to Josh and his family Ryan's preoperative email to his brother Chad (quoted above) Josh uttered: "… took the words right out of my mouth." Their commingling spirits are symbolized in the "coincidental" appearances of a silver VW "bug" at significant times and places after Ryan's death to which I allude in my "Journal of Grieving." Josh owned and loved a similar model of this rare collector's edition Volkswagen automobile.

This communion overflowed to their parents. The day before Ryan was pronounced dead, Cindy, his mom, was to exclaim : "Wouldn't it be wonderful if Ryan's lungs could be given to Josh!"

Jimeyer losing at backgammon to Josh Sheldon

Though he died ten weeks after Ryan, the precariousness of Josh's condition clouded the events of summer.

Yvette LeFlore, RN, Clinical Manager of the Cystic Fibrosis program documented in a memorandum to Len, Josh's father:

… Josh was admitted into Harper Hospital at the Detroit Medical Center on 7/12/02 and remains in the hospital as of this date (7/17/02). At approximately 11:30 P.M. 7/11/02 Josh started throwing up huge amounts of blood from his lungs. 911 had to be called to take him to a local hospital (Beaumont Hospital in Troy, MI) to stabilize him and make arrangements for transfer to DMC. This was a very acute occurrence in which a very large amount of blood was brought up. His heart rate was also very elevated during this crisis i.e. approximately from 160-180. On Friday 7/12/02 Josh underwent another embolization to seal off blood vessels that had burst…

And Dr. Dana Kissner, his CF pulmonologist, was to record later in Josh's medical chart:

HOSPITAL COURSE: The patient had an extremely stormy hospital course. He was brought emergently to interventional radiology for bronchial artery embolization. They found a single abnormal bronchial artery with branches to the right and left lung fields, which were embolized with PVA. The procedure was difficult because of the patient's severe respiratory insufficiency.

When he returned to the unit, he was inextremitus, gasping for breath and oxygenating very poorly. Decisions previously had been made to attempt to forego intubation and mechanical ventilation because of poor results with this particular disease. For this reason, the patient was treated conservatively with Solu-Medrol, morphine sulfate, Ativan and non-invasive ventilatory support with BIPAP. The morphine was given at first IV push and then by a patient activated pump. The patient was placed on 100% (oxygen). At this point, another discussion was held with the patient's parents along with Father Jim Meyer….

Lynne, his mom, Len and I, along with the medical team worked for five hours to stabilize him. I wrote Ryan a more graphic description of what the three of us did.

… we alternated putting pressure on the surgical packing on his groin, so he wouldn't blow it open when he coughed, which had happened before, while another gave him a neck rub or did visualization to help him relax, while another wiped the sweat off his face and neck …while another gave him sips of water, while two of us held the urinal while he peed out the water and then gave him Ensure to drink--- then the emesis basin when he hurled out the Ensure…

Ryan's email response could be predicted. "Josh is one heck of an amazing kid. Wow… two people to hold the urinal. Makes me jealous!"

What I beheld in the room that night was Michelangelo's *"Pieta"*. Mother, Mary soothing and caressing her bruised and broken son --- gasping for life.

Lynne was to reflect afterwards:

At this moment I knew it was a privilege to be Josh's Mom. It was as though at his weakest moment I was given strength and power to help him regain control. I was overwhelmed in knowing why God chose me with His guidance, to handle a dying child. …. A calm came over me as I wrapped my arms around my baby, pressing my cheek against his. It was as if we became one. I needed to convey peacefulness. I needed to remove him from the chaos, pain and panic he was experiencing…. (The complete text will be found in the Epilogue.)

Meanwhile Josh's only sibling, Jennifer Mervak, pregnant at home with her young family entreated to no one in particular and to the world:

FIGHTING FOR BREATH

He sits hunched over on the hospital bed.
I've never seen this look of pain on his face before.
Breathing is laborious, every breath is a struggle
Coughing a noise that makes strangers turn their heads.

A noise so familiar to me.

Thick, green, sticky mucus spit into a cup
Disgusting to others, a triumph to us.

I listen to the doctor's words.
I fight back the tears
I pray to God,
Please help him.
Please give him a new set of lungs!

My mind jumps and spins.
Why aren't more people organ donors?
How many sets of good lungs
Have been buried in the dirt to rot
Since my brother's been listed.

My baby brother. Twenty-four.
Struggling to breathe like he's ninety-nine.

I Loved a Boy

Though out of chronological sequence, I have included Josh's funeral homily here to fill in the picture of the man. As a priest, it is my ultimate professional gift to him and his family.

Funeral Homily for Josh Sheldon
November 7, 2002
Christ Lutheran Church,
Sterling Heights, Michigan

My name is Fr. James L. Meyer and I am a Catholic priest with the Archdiocese of Detroit. I would answer more quickly however, if you call me "Jimeyer", one word. It is an honor and a privilege to be here at Christ Lutheran Church. From the get-go when we talked last Monday evening at the Sheldon's there was instant rapport between Pastor Boone and myself.

Josh Sheldon and I have "run" with each other since at age nine, he was a bright enthusiastic little camper in my patrol at Onkoi Benek, the summer camp for kids with cystic fibrosis. I have watched with satisfaction as he grew from child to collegian to young adult. And then I have observed with dismay, as he went from healthy and active, to oxygen dependent --- first only at nighttime, then, in this life --- forever.

Only on Monday, I found out that seven months ago Josh had drawn up a Last Will and Testament. One page, Josh-terse, right to the point. "At my funeral": he began, " I would like it to be a celebration of my life, not a mourning of my death." Indeed, I trust all of you will feel in your hearts the Josh Sheldon you have known and loved, as I present but a snippet of his personality from some of my experiences with him.

.

I Loved a Boy

The next line of his Will blew me away: "I would also like Jimeyer to say a few nice words for me to make me look good!" WHAT AN OPPORTUNITY! Josh, haven't you learned even in death? --- paybacks are hell!

Pranks and counter-pranks have added color to the beautiful tapestry that has been our relationship. And now my turn to retaliate for the perfectly executed, rapier, needle-work job he did on me within this past month. There I am on Sunday afternoon, with him in his bedroom, to take his money, I mean play euchre with him --- and his pager goes off. This is the pager from University of Wisconsin Hospital at Madison. The only reason it would beep is that he was being called for his double-lung transplant. He grabs his telephone.

My heart rate soared. "Yes, this is Josh Sheldon," was his cool and controlled response. "Mom! Dad!" he called convincingly. In rushed Len and Lynne, the latter with a curious grin on her face as I now recall. "How much time do we have?" Josh continued into the phone. "Will there be room on the plane for my friend, Jimeyer? " My mind raced as fast as my heart --- "O god, what do I have on my calendar this week?" I said to myself. My fingers dug into Lynne's back. I am on the verge of bursting into ecstatic tears of joy.

Then Josh hands me the phone --- the dead phone --- where there had been no one on the other end ---- and looks me right in the face, with this silly, silly grin. "Gotcha", he announced in triumph!

Now I contend that that was the cruelest, nastiest prank of all. I protest, I didn't deserve it. Well there was the occasion in May of last year. The Sheldon Family had decided to vacation at Chalfonte House for a week.

150

Admittedly, the rents did increase significantly, but that was because of the extensive renovations to my 121 year old Victorian home in Elk Rapids Michigan. When not rented, this was a frequent haunt for Josh and a lot of other kids and parents. There is a newspaper article about it; copies of which I trust will be available after church. Josh prominently graces the front-page photo. Josh had done the architectural drawings for these renovations, but as rental season approached, construction had not been quite completed.

On May 4, 2001, I get this email from him: "Hey Jimeyer, any GOOD news on progress to the house???" This was to be an email with an attitude! I must admit I might have played a small part in precipitating the nasty missive. I had given him the "bad news- good news" routine the previous week. "Dear Josh, bad news is that both kitchens are incomplete. Good news is, we have a brand new outdoor BBQ grill. Bad news is we don't have functioning bathrooms -good news; the porta-johns are only a five minute walk away at the public park."

This might have gotten to him as he continued: "I have to warn you, you will be in very big trouble if we get up there and that place is a mess. This is my family's ONLY vacation this year and if it's wrecked because of you, consider yourself a goner! I have tried to explain to these people that these are important changes being made to beautify Chalfonte House, but they don't seem to understand. And they really don't understand paying ritzy resort prices for a dump! We understand if you discount accordingly. Well, talk to you soon. Have a great day. Josh."

WHAT THE CRAP? I darted off an email reply. "Yada yada yada. You tell your family that if they want ritzy accommodations, they can go out and buy ritzy sleeping bags to bring with them." But the best was yet to come. With my idea man and co-conspirator, Paul, here is what they found when the family arrived to commence their vacation on that warm Saturday afternoon in June. The house was cordoned completely in police barrier tape. Orange cones graced every entranceway and an officious volunteer fire fighter, with his walky-talky blaring, barred them from admission. "Electrical fire, can't use the place, --- for at least three days", he bellowed.

"Oh brother ---O brother", Josh lamented in his characteristic distress call. "Do you think this might be one of Jimeyer's pranks"? Lynne offered innocently? "Not even Jimeyer would be THIS cruel", was Josh's desperate cry. YES! YES! I trumpeted when the story was relayed to me in a subsequent phone call.

Let your own smiling and comforting thoughts of him continue to surface as I recount a couple more Josh memories.

I'm told about the day before his high school graduation party. He had his head completely shorn of his golden locks, the pride of his mother. When she saw her bald son, she wailed: "You look like you have cancer! And I'm a one disease mom!"

Mark Schwartz could tell this one better than I. Ever the polite one, Josh would always send a proper "Thank you" card. He did so after being treated to a steak dinner for his 21st birthday. I don't even want to know what else transpired on that memorable occasion, but the card to his benefactors read in part: ." .. oh yes, and I am very sorry for having deposited the $25.00 steak dinner --- on your backyard lawn."

I Loved a Boy

In response to one of those pervasive email questionnaires, beginning, "List your favorites", Josh answered this way to the question: "What is your favorite sound"? "All the sounds of nature, like when you're in the middle of a golf course and the birds are chirping and the wind is blowing and the rivers are a flowing, stuff like that." Does this not hearken back to early childhood walks, hand in hand with grandpa? A grandpa who had all the answers to a young boy's questions about trees and flowers, birds and stars?

"Celebrate my life, not mourn my death", was Josh's mandate to me. My issue is not: "How can I do this?", but rather, "How can I not do it!" Here is one who drank deeply of life, though the hemlock of cystic fibrosis had filled his cup since birth. And like the Master to whom he swore allegiance, it was a cup not chosen, but rather embraced out of love for others.

This giant, who even while tethered to his bed, with meds that filled a notebook, a 24-hour external breathing machine called BIPAP, and a constant morphine pump, could bring smiles to our hearts and prank me in a manner that scoffed in the teeth of death. Josh, my well-loved friend, I kneel at your feet, grateful to one who teaches me how to live --- instructs me how to love, --- and models for me, how to die.

I speak for all who are in this church and the myriad others upon whom you have cast your gigantic mantle of affection and courage. We treasure the many embraces and the exquisite love you have for all of us you call "family and friends." Even though in these latter weeks, we had to tiptoe through the maze of tubes and lines, being careful not to dislodge you from your life support, you willingly permitted us to proclaim our love for you.

And you replied in kind, and with levity. It is clear to family and close friends, that the struggles of awaiting your transplant in these past few months, were borne out of love for us more than for the vague possibility of personal gain for you.

The familiar words of St. Paul in I Corinthians, 13:2 come crashing home to me and to all of us who knew you. "If (I am) <u>without</u> love, <u>I am nothing at all.</u>" This is not a statement about utility; it is a statement about <u>existence</u>. The quintessential meaning of this passage is that without love, without loving, <u>I DO NOT EXIST</u>!

Though Paul directed these words to the Christian community, he meant them to have universal application. For him there was no difference between being an authentic human and an authentic Christian. Is not this at the heart of your attraction, our beloved Joshua? Is this not your ever-present gentle gift to us?

Not only did you talk these sacred words of inspiration, but even with your labored breathing, your vulnerability, you walked us through it all, giving us the opportunity of more abundant life. We can, therefore, sing together the psalmist's words you had adopted as your own as you pledged your love to God and all of us:

"I am God's delight and heart's desire. It is thus that I celebrate God's presence in my life and world. O God, You put into my hands gifts to relay to others. You entrust me with tasks far beyond my human abilities and empower me as Your son and servant destined to accomplish Your purposes amongst the peoples of this

world. It is no wonder that I love You, O God." (Psalm 18: adapted by Pastor Leslie F. Brandt - readapted by JLM)

And then in your final night with us with your exhausted body, you confessed to your mom your sadness at being so prepared to die and not doing so. "I was so peaceful and it felt so good." But you, ever the gentle and considerate man, saw the sorrow in our eyes that Saturday night. "You need to help me to die", you whispered to your mother in her arms. "Permission?' "Yes" was your reply. "You have permission from dad and me", she sighed. It was about 3:00 AM. Within but a few hours time, you peacefully breathed your last, embraced by mom and dad and surrounded by persons who love you.

And your heart and soul sang out with vibrant unsuffocated voice: "The traumatic experiences of this life cannot destroy me, O God. You have granted me a security that I could never find among the things of this world. You have eased from my life the fear of death. What follows the grave is not my fearful concern. For you are a God who is concerned about me. God who has reached into my distraught life to heal my wounds. God who encompasses me with eternal love." (Ibid.)

And let the church pray, AMEN!

Chapter 27: Of Friends and Kin

As we speak of heroes, saints and angels, a wondrous paradox textures these stories and these lives. Tim Burgess expressed it best. "To me," Tim confided, "Ryan was no hero; he was a best friend." While not denying the former, it is the latter that permits their spirits to emerge within us. Heroes, saints and angels are awfully hard to follow, but friends and kin can walk beside us always.

Ryan Upgrade v1.5 proclaimed his email for 7/29/02.

> Now that I have all the information, figured I'd pass it along to you. Nice huh? TOMORROW, Tuesday, July 30, at 11:30 a.m., I will be having some minor surgery to try and correct the problem of my right eye not being able to close. … They are going to place a small gold weight in the eye lid to bring it down…. Either way, this isn't a big major deal, that's why it didn't make it to Ryan version 2. … So please be thinking of me, praying for me, sending me cards, sending me money, the usual stuff. If you only do one, please do the money bit. Thanks! Ryan.

… and returning home on July 31:

> Surgery went very good…. On a side note, I also have a 'boob' on my head where my right ear used to be. It's a plastic curved covering so that I can lay on my side without irritating my ear. (where they had removed some cartilage to repair the eye lid). It's nice and all, but I like it better when boobs come in pairs. …

"Geez Ryan," I chided throughout the summer, especially in the company of others: "You're taking Botox, (for relief of his neck pain), you have a 'Boy Band' haircut (Ryan wrote to Emily in January: 'I have always wanted Shane West's hair! Thank you, Emcare for turning me from dud to stud.') and you have a golden ball. What more could a boy ask for?"

August 6 we traveled to Chalfonte House together on what was to be his body's last visit there. Tears well up as I read his parting entry in the guest book on August 17.

Jimeyer, What an adventure this past week and one half have been! Even though I felt pretty crappy the whole time, and really didn't get any sleep, I managed to enjoy some special time in this special place with some special people. I needed this week so much. To be around such caring people is what life is all about....

Chapter 28: Ryan Dies

The pain screams from the depth of my disconsolate soul:

Thursday, August 22, 2002 9:07 p.m. Subject: Ryan, 'The Scammer" Giannini:

You cannot believe how very, very difficult it is for me to write this memo to you. It is through copious tears that I inform you that Ryan is at this moment struggling for life in the critical care unit of Beaumont Hospital in Troy, MI. Last evening, after Ry and I had spoken on the phone about his (continuing) difficulty breathing, he was taken to Troy Beaumont Hospital. It turned out that his oxygen saturation was seventy-nine (one hundred is what is desired). He quickly recouped with a four liter flow of oxygen, through a nasal canula, and with the help of Vicodin, spent a restful night.

At 11 a.m. this morning, while Cindy and I were watching him sleep, he stopped breathing. A code blue was called. He was stabilized and admitted to the critical care unit. There was some evidence of fixed and dilated pupils --- and some involuntary movement, early in the afternoon. The neurological surgeon gave a more hopeful report at 5 p.m., but by the time I left at 7 p.m.,.I could detect only a suspicion of voluntary movement. The doctor said the usual 'seventy-two hours will tell.' PLEASE LIFT ALL OF US UP IN YOUR PRAYERS, LOVE AND SPIRIT. Love, Jimeyer

The first e-mail response was from one whom Ryan had described as: "one of my bestest friends in the whole world." I was charged to read it at the bedside. It was the plaintive distant plea of Tim Burgess in Denver to a comatose Ryan in Detroit. This is boy-to-boy and man-to-man; a candid heart's concern from one who as a kid experienced the awful terror of a diagnosis of osteosarcoma and just turned seventeen, the amputation of his leg above the knee. It is the pleading prayer of one whose kinship was bonded to the other in the kiln of childhood human suffering. From that awful depth, he wrote:

> Ryan: When I first read that you were in the hospital my first instinct was to try to figure out how I could possibly get to you to show you how much I care, and just generally be there for you.... Maybe it is just an unspoken bond between us that you know how much I truly care about you, and how big a part of my life you are, but it can't hurt to tell you. I cherish every conversation we have whether it be spiritual, political, perverted, or just about nothing at all...You are a best friend in every sense of the word, and I love you for it.. Tim

Meanwhile helpless lamentation from the other end of the country. His friend and confidant, Scott Brinkman, having returned to his home in Stowe, Vermont after spending the August days with Ryan, could only cry out from the pain of his separation: "Oh Shit !!!" Eloquent words of concern and compassion bringing consolation to us all.

Two days later I would send the following message I am including here in its entirety:

> I can hardly think or see coherently through my tears, as I try to send you this terrible message. My heart has not been so devastated since September 6, 1988 when my beloved Andrew Peter was killed on his bicycle at age 21.

159

I Loved a Boy

At 7:30 a.m., today, Saturday, August 24, 2002, Ryan Giannini was pronounced 'brain dead' at Troy Beaumont hospital. Characteristic of some hospitals and medical professionals, they insist on a corroborative proclamation twelve hours later. Most of the rest of us understand that 'brain dead' is dead. Ryan was twenty years old.

Those of you who know me, clearly understand that in the time I have known him, Ryan has successfully taken a huge chunk of my heart and melded it with his own. Though undeserving of the love of one so heroic, I cherish every moment of that love. And knowing it was mutual consoles me.

Again, as was his way of planning, whether wittingly or not, Ry choreographed the events leading to his death. He successfully parlayed his most recent surgery to enable him to spend almost two weeks at Chalfonte House with the friends with whom he was the closest. Last Sunday he hosted his church youth group and then spent three days with his family at a cottage in Canada.

I just 'happened' to call him last Wednesday evening --- fifteen minutes after the family had returned. He told me that his breathing difficulties continued and he was considering admission to the hospital. Later that night, his dad, Rich, called to tell me his oxygen saturation rate upon admission was seventy-nine --- quickly brought to one hundred through four liter flow of O_2 (oxygen) by nasal canula.

Cindy, his mom, stayed with him through the night. Was it a vision or an omen when she awakened therein and saw his countenance, radiant and peaceful. He gave her the 'thumbs up' and she returned to sleep.

I Loved a Boy

When I arrived at 11 a.m. on Thursday, August 22,
2002, (his brother, Chad's twenty-third birthday) I
observed him sitting up in bed asleep, but breathing
easily. I did not want to awaken him. Within five
minutes, while Cindy and I were sitting watching him,
Cindy exclaimed: "He's not breathing!" Neither of us
could arouse him and a 'Code Blue' ensued.

It was later determined that he was without oxygen to
the brain for fifteen to twenty minutes. From that time
on, aside from some response in the pupils of his eyes, I
detected no intentional movement.

As was his and his parents wishes, 'Gift of Life' has
been called to determine whether any of his organs
might be able to continue his life here on earth in
someone else. Skin, bone and lungs are unlikely, given
his disease, but hopefully others.

Because of this, funeral plans remain unmade. The
emptiness I feel is immeasurable. Alternately, I feel
calmed and sustained by his great spirit within me.
Please hold up all of us at this time in your prayers,
thoughts and hearts. Much love, Jimeyer.

Subsequent reflection: The family and I have often mused
about "what if?" --- he had died at Chalfonte? -- or in
Canada? --- or in the middle of the night? --- alone?
Instead he died in circumstances wherein all the medical
interventions possible were accessible.

The last words written by Ryan Giannini – on a tee shirt from the collection with Jimeyer's college graduation photo which Paul Hresko had distributed to the older campers in August, 2002.

Chapter 29: Journal of Grieving: Introduction

Determined to keep the memory of this great soul alive and publicized throughout the world, I kept a journal of my raw and unadorned feelings commencing with the day Ryan was declared dead. I planned to do so for a hundred days, but at the end of sixty, I felt no need to write further. My reflections include irrational feelings. They may be hurtful to some. They are not pretty, even to me. In my profession I have learned that feelings are illogical. One cannot be blamed because of them. I entreat the reader not to hold my feet too close to the fire because of my insensitivities.

I have been a grief counselor for over a third of a century. The most difficult circumstances involve the death of a child. I am a certified social worker with specialization in this area. I am a badge-bearing chaplain and card-carrying clergyman. I know what to say and what not to say ---with emphasis upon the latter. One's best offer is a willingness to walk with parents, grandparents, siblings, family and friends in silence on their awful pilgrimages.

My vocation as a clergyperson calls me to be a believer. One might presume that the motto for my ministry would be taken from the Bible. It is not. My guiding principle imprinted on a faded poster above my desk is a saying from Albert Camus: *"Don't walk before me, I may not follow; don't walk behind me, I may not lead; just walk beside me and be my friend."*

I have not aborted my grieving by cocooning it in the cliché-consolation of "heaven," "a happier place," "no more pain," "at rest now," or even "he's with God." These may bring comfort later. For the present, I share the raw feelings that have spilled out from the depth of a disconsolate soul. I have thought unpleasant and forbidden thoughts as well as been given unbelievable insights. I have changed the names of the some of the characters and places. Identifying them is irrelevant to the message.

Rosita Kintz and her family
Marcus Kintz, Rosita Kintz, Stephenie Kintz, Lori Fortino-Franklin and Alan Franklin

I present myself from the depth of my being, not to be emulated but to help free you, the reader, for whatever you might feel on your awful journey of loss. Sharing my feelings may make your pilgrimage of pain more tolerable. It's more than a question of *"misery loves company,"* rather, to paraphrase another common saying, *"many hearts make work light"*. You need no one's permission, certainly not mine, to feel what you feel in your grieving. I tell my story with hope that bitterness evolves into wholeness as it has with me.

Please ponder: "Here's a trained, experienced counselor and clergyman who is having similar thoughts and feelings as I. The anger, the irrationality, even the hopelessness and despair. I guess it's all right for me to feel these feelings and think these thoughts." My friend, Rosita Kintz, who within a period of ten years had a husband, a sister and a daughter die of cancer as well as two other children die from cystic fibrosis, comforted me in a note which read in part: "The hurt of separation is so great for a while, but it will take you to the most holiest of places --- if you let it."

My *Journal* begins with the solitary walk from Ryan's bedside, through the lobby to the parking structure. I had to leave the hospital without him. My edited reflections comprise the next thirteen chapters. May they bring you comfort. May you discover hope in the meaning of the life of your loved one to integrate her or him into your living today and tomorrow.

Chapter 30: Journal of Grieving: The Agony Begins

Saturday, August 24, 2002:

It is outrageous that cars are moving, activities continuing, people, parents and kids are walking, talking, laughing and playing. That they remain alive is unfair. How can they live on? Don't they realize that Ryan is dead? --- this enormous soul who had filled the world with every kind of emotion from frivolous to sublime.

How can his family and I talk and laugh --- and most of all, eat? I never again want to eat --- to honor this enormous soul who returned my love a hundredfold. I never again want to see the inside of this hospital!

As Rich, his father, said before I fled at my end of the evening, "He less and less looks like Ryan."

His face is ashen and his blank stare more and more distant as they cover him with a "warming blanket." With impersonal clinical precision they draw blood and suck other fluids from his body while at the same time infusing him. It is macabre as they make frantic phone calls and prepare to cut him up to divide and distribute him throughout the region. God, I need to believe that he has so distanced himself that he is no longer privy to this heinous affair.

I hate leaving this hospital without my arms around the shoulders of my beloved Ryan. I am undeserving of all that he has given me; no it is true, it is not false humility. I lament like Rachel whose children are no more. I sob at the void left by one so beautiful, whom I can embrace no more nor whisper to him once again: "Ryan, if you ever knew how much I love you, you would be embarrassed"; to hear him murmur in reply: "I love you too."

O God, please create an eternity where once again we may embrace! Where we can smirk and laugh out loud at the one final intimate gift that he gave me in death which shall remain forever a secret between us.

Sunday, August 25:

Sunday was a day of up and down feelings. I relaxed on a half hour's walk in Lafayette Park near the center city of Detroit where I live. I received needed support from the Upsons and the Chalfonte kids. Noon until 10 p.m. was spent with the Giannini family at three major meetings.

The first funeral planning meeting with "Fr. John", "Audrey", his Associate, (not their real names) Ry's parents and siblings, droned on. Such trivia! I cannot believe that Chad and Jill, who sat motionless through two grueling hours, will continue in active support of this kind of church nonsense. The miniscules of the pedestrian planning drove me up a wall. Perhaps it bothered only me. Everyone else seemed to go along with the program.

The trifling, endless, serious discussion of how the chicken for the funeral luncheon should be cooked! And at that moment, our beloved, our darling, the value of his viscera having been assessed, was being carved up and distributed. I wanted to shout at Audrey to take the friggin' chicken and kielbasa and shove them up her ass!

I am grateful beyond measure that Fr. John, the pastor, who controls these matters, proffered that I preach the homily/eulogy. Rich concurred. He wanted me from the beginning. Cindy sat silent, but affirming. I understand her hesitancy. She felt it would be too hard on me. But this is what I do best as a priest. It is my personal and professional gift. Ryan's homily would be the last tribute I could give before his body was returned to ashes.

Heightened anxiety. I have to "reduce" Ryan to two services, a "Sharing Service" the night before, then the funeral homily. I am privileged, but beginning to panic. I need to apologize for my impatience at the planning session I directed at home with the family. I don't leave the Giannini's till late Sunday. I return home to my apartment in Detroit--- alone. It is dark. Ryan peers at me around every corner as I move from room to room. No time tonight to start putting the services together. I am exhausted, but not tired.

Monday, August 26:

Monday morning up at dawn, cutting and pasting from copious notes what I want to put in either service. Chad and I talk about the music and burning a CD. My attorney colleague, Ken Prather, asks his wife who agrees to retype the lyrics. Mary Enright, my dear friend who is executive secretary to the head of Hutzel Hospital, volunteers to print three hundred copies of the music. I want to complete the Tuesday evening service, so I can concentrate on the all-important homily for Wednesday's funeral.

Because I have neither service completed, I will be unable to stay all day to wake Ryan. The family needs their private time, but so do I. I arrive at the funeral home at 2:30 p.m. Family visitation is at 2 p.m.; for others, from 3 to 9 p.m.. Immediate family has not yet arrived. I leave shortly after 3

168

p.m. and return in the evening. Tuesday night's Sharing Service is complete, but it leaves me uncertain.

It is wrong to say that "Ryan looked good" in the casket. Loneliness and emptiness are setting in. I am not pleased with the services. I am inadequate in conveying how I feel and in capturing the giant that he was. I don't want him to be gone --- even from the funeral home. He will be cremated. That's good; his ashes will be around. It is going to be hard. RYAN I LOVE YOU VERY MUCH.

After visitation I return to my apartment at 10:30 p.m. It is good to have Mara Timlin, a Chalfonte kid, drive me home.

Tuesday, August 27:

I have neither listened to the radio nor watched television since last Thursday. There is no worthwhile news except Ryan. My taste for food is returning and I begrudge that it is. Ryan cannot eat. Hmmmmmmm he hasn't eaten for ten years! I smile.

I prayed to Ryan last night to help me sleep and to inspire me to communicate to the congregation his message of faith and love. I awoke at 3:30 a.m. after five hours of sleep. I wrote reflections for the homily for the next hour and a half. Returning to bed, I slept off and on until seven then arose more refreshed than I have been since last Thursday.

Creation of the homily begins. I feel as if the upper right quadrant of my heart is gone. On rare occasions I write every word of a service: one- to insure I won't ramble off on tangents, two - to present a complete portrait, and three - to have a lasting tribute for someone special.

Preparation is labored. I type for five and a half hours. I have said enough to capture Ry and "just end it." Re-editing is time consuming but finally the homily is "in the can." I remain uncertain about the service tonight ---it sounds foreign.

I arrive at the funeral home at 4 p.m.. WHERE IS EVERYONE? DOES NOT THE WORLD REALIZE THAT RYAN HAS DIED? Why isn't the funeral home packed to overflowing? Where are all MY friends and support? For the ensuing two hours, three dozen people sprinkle in. I am bummed.

THE SHARING SERVICE WAS SPLENDID! It lasted from 7:30 p.m. past 9:30 p.m.. The place was packed to overflowing. I am grateful Mara drove me home once again. Having Ryan and Emily Upson and Mara living in the "hood" comforts me.

Chapter 31: Journal of Grieving: Ryan's funeral

Wednesday, August 28:

It is the day of the funeral. I take the opportunity to review and "time" the homily. Twenty-five minutes -- fine. In attempting to control my emotions I fear my delivery will sound too much like a "reading".

The service begins. Never before have I witnessed a "sprinkling rite" where everyone is invited to process to the open casket at the front of church to sprinkle the body. I absorb every moment of it, with melancholy, as I recalled Erin Arbogast's recent dream she shared at last night's service:

In the basement of Chalfonte house, also the familiar stage for gaming nights of "gangster", is a tree painted on the wall where every Chalfonte kid writes their name on a leaf and the date of their first stay --- forever imprinting them in the fullness of life.

My dream began with everyone from Chalfonte week II and Memorial Day weekends gathered around Ryan in the steam shower bathroom. Scott Brinkman (staff) handed each of us paint and a paintbrush, and together we painted our names in brilliant colors and styles all over Ryan's arms, back and chest. When we were finished, he was a luminous rainbow.

In silence, the dream shifted down the road to the beach and I watched Ryan walk with ease into the water --- cloaked in our names. He walked beyond that shallow pier of stones where the water folds over the point in rhythmic V's --- a favorite place to walk and take photos. He walked out as I have seen him do so many summers-before, but this time, with our colors and our names, Ryan walked into Lake Michigan until he was gone. The waters parted and returned polished smooth by memories – graciously accepting this precious gift.

In contrast, I chuckle to myself seeing his water-soaked tee shirt and recalling the earlier-told Chalfonte House event when he attempted to orchestrate a "wet tee shirt contest" which was aborted by "The Management." Today he got his wish -- partially.

I have included my last best gift to Ryan in its entirety, my homily at his funeral service . It was well received. Jon Piercey's comment afterwards heartens me. As we embraced he whispered: "Jimeyer, I could listen to you till the end of the day." And Erin's: "Ryan's passing has left me turning like a broken kaleidoscope. Jimeyer, you gleamed before the church today – your colors, your laughter, your pain and tears."

Theme: *"This treasure we possess is in earthen vessels, to make it clear that its surpassing power comes from God and not from us." (2 Corinthians 4:7).*

My name is Fr. James Meyer and I have been a priest of the Archdiocese of Detroit in relatively good standing for over forty-two years. My friends better know me as "Jimeyer", one word. For the past three decades the ministry that has been closest to my heart, is to critically and terminally ill children and youth, especially those with cystic fibrosis, regardless of race or religious affiliation.

By the family's wishes and that of Fr. John, the pastor, I have been chosen to give the homily. I am honored

I Loved a Boy

and more grateful to them than they will ever know. Now a "homily" is not a eulogy, it is a commentary on the Scriptures and application to our lives. The Catholic Church frowns on eulogies as a part of the funeral rites. I agree.

However, it always has struck me that each and every one of us here this morning, including all of us ministers, would <u>not</u> be here except for the deceased. To put it more bluntly, if Ryan Giannini had not died, this church would be <u>empty</u> at this hour. Look around you. It is <u>filled,</u>

It is filled to celebrate Ryan's new relationship with the Lord. But more than that. <u>Ryan</u> already knows what that's about. Therefore this service is especially for <u>us</u>, centered on him. To me it makes ultimate good sense that this scriptural homily not be some doctrinal treatise, however edifying, but rather, how "The Word" was lived out in Ryan's life. This I intend to do, notwithstanding how inadequate I feel to fulfill this honor.

I have held dozens, perhaps hundreds of children in my arms when they've died. All of them have been special to me, --- some closer than others. Among them all, save one, Ryan is first in my love and in my heart. I am humbled to be listed in his obituary as "close friend." Mentally multiply those words as far as you are able, and you will glimpse at its reality. Those who know Ryan, and me, know that it is true.

In the Gospel of Matthew, chapter 25, verses thirty-one and following, we heard:

'At the appointed time, the Lord will come in glory, escorted by all the angels of heaven...He will say... "Come,

173

you blessed of Abba God! Inherit the kindom (sic)
prepared for you from the creation of the world!
For I was hungry and you fed me. I was thirsty and you
gave me drink. I was a stranger and you welcomed me,
naked and you clothed me. I was ill and you comforted me;
in prison and you came to visit me." "When did we see you
like this?" they inquired. "The truth is, every time you did
this for the least of my sisters and brothers --- you did it for
me."'

This gospel text is especially dear to Rich, Ryan's
father. More than once over the last few days he has been
eloquent in pointing out how perfect this is for Ryan's life.
He suggests for example, that the terms "food and drink,
nakedness, strangers and the imprisoned" extend far
beyond the apparent meaning of those words. I agree and
recommend that, armed with your personal knowledge of
Ryan, you mediate on this text from Matthew 25 after you
get home.

Not unrelated to the above, I smile as I recall an
incident that occurred at Chalfonte House a couple of
years ago. Ryan was "chef's assistant" and assigned to
peeling and preparing vegetables. As he went about his
task in his precise manner, I made the fatal mistake, of
suggesting <u>how</u> he should do it. He put down his paring
knife, looked straight ahead, sighed, then turned to me with
exasperation and said: "Whose driving?" Enough said.

When <u>I</u> think of Ryan and the Scriptures, I am filled
with the life and words of St. Paul. In second Corinthians,
chapter 12, (verses 7b-10) Paul proclaims: "<u>I</u> was given a
thorn in <u>my</u> flesh --- a messenger of Satan, to beat me --- to
keep me from exalting myself. Three times I begged God
that it might leave me. And God said to me, 'My grace is
sufficient for you, <u>for power is perfected in weakness.'</u>

"Most gladly, therefore", Paul continues, "I would rather boast about my weaknesses, that the power of Christ may dwell in me." Think of Ryan. "<u>So I am content with weakness, ... when I am powerless, it is then that I am strong." (repeat)</u> . Think of Ryan.

And I am reminded of Ry's award winning essay entitled "Beating the Odds", written in the eleventh grade at Stevenson High School. It begins, "Some people think that when the odds are against them, they should cash in their chips and call it quits." ... it continues: "The odds that I am overcoming is my so-called 'disability.' I have Gorham's Syndrome." ... the essay ends: "As for me, I may back down from some situations, but not without giving it my best shot first. Because no matter what cards life throws at me, I will come out a winner, and beat the odds."

We know Ryan's favorite tee shirt. (Here in church, I won't even mention his other favorites.) He was laid out in it. The frog grabbing the pelican's neck as the frog is being swallowed. The caption announces: "Don't Ever Give Up!" And Paul instructs us: "When I am powerless, it is then that I am strong." Think of Ryan.

All of us are familiar with Paul's eloquent words about love. The text from portions of chapters twelve and thirteen of I Corinthians is used in the majority of Christian marriages. It announces: "Strive for greater gifts", then continues,

> *"If I <u>speak"</u> (pause) - think of Ryan –" in the tongues of mortals and angels, but do not have love, I am a noisy gong or a clanging cymbal.*

> *And if I have prophetic powers, and understand all mysteries, and all knowledge and if I have all*

175

faith so as to remove mountains, but do not have love, I am nothing.

If I give away all my possessions and hand over my body so that I may boast, but do not have love, I gain nothing.

<u>*Love is patient; love is kind.*</u>
Love is not envious or boastful or arrogant or rude. It does not insist on its own way, it is not irritable or resentful; it does not rejoice in wrongdoing, but rejoices in the truth.

It bears all things, believes all things, hopes all things, endures all things.

*Love never ends." **(Revised Standard Version)***

*In struggling with his decision to undergo corrective surgery, it seems to me Ryan had three major reasons to "go for it." **1.** To improve his looks, therefore attract chicks. **2.** To enable him to eat once again. And **3.** To speak and be heard. I don't believe that the majority of us faced with a similar decision would have his choice as <u>our</u> No. 1. Ry had a lot to say, and wanted to be heard. As to eating, he adapted to his tube feeding. As to looks, it was "take me as I am."*

I recall as we were driving to Josh's to play euchre just prior to his February 12th major surgery, I turned to him and said: "Your dad told me that they are also going to do something to fix your nose?" He turned to me and deadpanned: "what's wrong with my nose?"

When speaking about this text at marriages, I point out that St. Paul really had <u>little</u> to say in describing what

love is. Most of what he says, speaks to what love is not.
Only two words say what it is...not my first choice, but then
I was not called upon to write the Scriptures. "Love is
patient, love is kind." "Patient": what we name hospital
clients and rightly so. The word comes from "patior"
which means, "to suffer." Paul in effect is telling us that
without the element of suffering, there can be no true love.

And "kind", comes from the Old English, "kin",
which means family, and by extension "being in
relationship with others." Think of the magnetism of this
heroic young man. He lived out this definition of love as
few others.

While on the subject of heroes, I want to say this. I
am dismayed at how cavalierly we attribute "hero" status
to those who in reality are victims --- perhaps being in the
wrong place when the time was wrong. . And we "medal"
those who've performed outstanding feats of "daring do."
While I might feel sympathy for the former and quietly
applaud the latter, neither measures up to my standards for
heroes.

Heroes are those who struggle--- I mean really
struggle --- day in and out --- with adversity, and force it
into submission, often with determination and maybe
humor. I might admire the incidental hero but for the one
who has the task of coping from the moment he awakens, if
indeed he was able to spend a restful night, I find it an
awesome privilege to kneel at his feet, in profound humility.
Again, I am reminded of Paul who says: "Be imitators of
me, not of Christ, but of ME. In effect he tells us: "you are
to be the Christ to those whom you encounter. Not an
abstract Jesus, even one risen from the dead, but it is you,
in whom He lives and breathes and has his being.

I Loved a Boy

Because you and I are so earthbound, we need the hand of one who is the same to guide us on our spiritual pathway. And Ryan did that for all of us --- with an outrageous sense of humor. As I sit at my computer, I glance over my shoulder at the first birthday gift I received from him --- a 14 pack of --- "Depends." Attached was a three-word note. "Just in case."

How frequently we have been recipients, shall I say "victims" of the perfect greeting card. At age seventeen, Tim Burgess, one his closest confidants, had an above-knee amputation secondary to osteosarcoma, bone-cancer. The day of his surgery Ry's card to him went something like this: "I trust you will be feeling well soon" (open card)." ... "and back on your <u>feet</u> again." "Feet" was crossed out ... and substituted --- was the word "foot." On Tim's 16th birthday, Ry had surprised him with --- a jump rope. You will have to ask Tim, Piecey or his other friends how it was wrapped. After all, we are still in church.

To bring community out of chaos and humor out of adversity in a manner so earthy is to call forth an authentic spirit of Christ we all can understand. Even his emails concerning his last corrective surgery, reading in part, "July 30th at 11:30 a.m., I will be having some "minor" surgery to try and correct the problem of my right eye not being able to close." He concludes: "so please be thinking of me, praying for me, sending me cards, sending me money, the usual stuff. If you only do one, --- please do the money bit."

Post-operatively he writes: "Yay! I'm home! Surgery went very good. ... On a side note, I also have a 'boob' on my head where my right ear used to be. It's a plastic covering so that I can lay on my side without irritating my ear. It's nice and all, but I like it better when boobs come in pairs."

Though we use the term loosely, humans are a different class of creatures than angels. I have to admit I would have a difficult time imitating an angel, because I am no angel. Nor was Ryan a "little angel." This brings us to the central text to which I encouraged you pay particular attention.

Think of how accurately 2 Corinthians, Chapter 4, verses 7-12 of St. Paul describe Ryan:

"But this treasure we possess is in earthen vessels, to make it clear that its surpassing power comes from God and not from us.

We are afflicted in every way possible, but we are not crushed. We are full of doubts, but we never despair. We are persecuted, but never abandoned. We are struck down, but never destroyed.

Continually we carry about in our bodies the death of Jesus, so that in our bodies the life of Jesus may also be revealed.

While we live, we are constantly being delivered to death for Jesus' sake, so that the life of Jesus may also be revealed in our bodies.

So then, death is at work in us, but <u>life is at work in you</u>" (emphasis added).

Realize that when St. Paul said "this treasure we possess is in earthen vessels"; he was not talking about some " clay pot." His analogy was to Greco-Roman wrestlers who performed in the buff. To make it more

179

difficult for them to be pinned, they covered themselves with grease or oil before the match. And their arena was dirt and sand. Soon into the match, imagine the ugly crust that caused their bodies to appear distorted. Then ponder the profound strength beneath their disfigurement.

Think of Ryan. Have Ry in mind as you listen. Of minor note, is his attraction to professional wrestling. He and the Chalfonte kids never allowed me to watch either "Smack Down" or "South Park; too risqué for me they asserted. Besides, I was not old enough. Again, think about the athletes, whose performance belies the hours of preparation beforehand.

Unless you lived with Ryan, you may be unaware of the hours that it took for him to get ready in the morning. It involved discontinuing his tube feedings, then an array of injections of appropriate medicines and fluids, clearing the secretions that persistently blocked his nose and mouth, and lately, the special delicate care of his eye and eyelid --- along with the routine toilet care familiar to all of us.

I cannot find in scripture a more appropriate description of Ryan Giannini. The text concludes: <u>*"but life is at work in you."*</u> *Ryan transmitted life. Ry displayed his love and we could never get enough of it. His family and his friends, his schoolmates and SOS (Students Offering Service), the Youth group of his Church, the Chalfonte kids, --- and me.*

Early on I learned the lesson of his meticulous morning ritual. This was after a few fatal errors in disrupting it. In these later years, whenever we stayed together, whether in Florida, Detroit, Elk Rapids, or elsewhere, once he got up in the morning, I would ignore him. When he was ready, he would present himself to me (arms open gesture).

I would enfold him in my arms, resting his misshapen head against my heart. "I love you, Ryan," I would say, often adding, "Ryan, if you knew how much I loved you, you would be embarrassed." He would reply, "I love you too." For these precious moments, it was the embrace of two souls, committed to being "with each other"; not the perfunctory embrace of two who do it out of custom while peering over their shoulders, impatient for their morning coffee.

Ours was a love built on genuine mutual respect and eagerness to learn from each other --- to claim as one's own, the strength we saw in the other. Isn't this after all, the community that St. Paul proclaims? "So then, death is at work in us, *but life is at work in you.*"

I conclude, not because I have nothing more to say, but because Rich is looking at his watch. Just kidding. Perhaps it is best that we depart, unfinished. Perhaps it is best that we leave untouched the memories that so many of us are holding in our hearts unmentioned. Perhaps that is the way it should be, so that this noble man can continue to unfold his love within us and among us.

A longtime friend wrote the following lines for me about another beloved one. These words sear my heart today as they did years ago. "But you see, it should be a tenet of faith --- not that we should die and rise, but that we should all die young, so as not to burden the world with wisdom come of living too long --- without ideals."

God bless you, Ryan.

After the funeral, I declare to Fr. John, the Pastor, Daniel, the Music Minister and others. "This two hour and fifteen minute ceremony was the finest funeral I have ever attended either as participant or spectator. If Ryan were king, president or other nobleman, he could not have been more honored."

As mandated by the pastor, every element of any service at his church is conducted with dignity, deliberateness and reflection. Notwithstanding, it was perfection --- with little passion! I pity them! I can do with a great deal of imperfection when the perfection is supplanted by passion. It is reported that the ancient Greeks were unaccustomed to writing obituaries for their noble men. They asked but one question concerning the deceased. *"Did he have passion?"*

Chapter 32: Journal of Grieving: Coincidences and Music

Early in my ministry I recall a mother of a deceased ten year old confiding that she had seen her daughter. "Father, I was not dreaming. It was the middle of the day and I was wide-awake. I talked to her and she to me. Am I going crazy?" she asked. I was inclined to agree with her assessment, until this turned out to be the first of similar conversations with many others.

I am convinced that encounters with deceased loved ones are both frequent and varied. They are unanticipated and unpredictable. Most can be dismissed as "coincidences." In counseling I emphasize that these are phenomena; special gifts to be savored. They come to many who have loved, while others who love just as deeply receive none.

I share my "coincidences" subsequent to Ryan's death without drawing conclusions as to ultimate source or meaning. This is what has happened and this is what it meant to me. I leave it for other experts in spirituality, psychology or thanatology to apply proper professional spin. As for me the aphorism resounds: "*If we don't listen, God doesn't hear.*"

I never dream about Ryan. He manifests his presence through tangible objects that have special significance, namely quarters. Let me explain.

He was a fanatic about money. For every board or card game at Chalfonte he would contrive a monetary payout, albeit nominal. With our most-played games of euchre and backgammon, the mandatory rule is: "*It is dimes until age sixteen, then it is quarters, FOR THE REST OF YOUR LIFE!"*

Since his death, quarters have "coincidentally" turned up in unexpected places so many times that, after the first several, though still consoling, their appearance has become unremarkable. I include some examples later in this chronicle.

Because of Ryan's compromised speech, his voice was the computer and his music. Of the hundreds of songs in his collection, I have chosen thirteen, arranged below in order of significance. These will be included in an "Ultimate Ryan Songs" CD, Chad hopes to produce.

1. ***"Canticle of the Sun"***

It is Ryan, when he had a clear resonant voice, singing into a tape recorder with all the gusto a five year old could muster.

"The heavens are telling the glory of God... come dance in the forest, come play in the fields..."

2. ***"Never Surrender"*** by Corey Hart

This song formed the bedrock for Ryan's life. It is not fortuitous that it was the first cut on the first CD's Ryan burned; also included on **"Ryan's Music *Special Release*: Music for the Heart, Mind, And Soul":**

"So, if you're lost and on your own, you can never surrender... and when the night is cold and dark, you can see ... 'cause no one can take away your right to fight and to never surrender."

3. *"I Hope You Dance"* by Lee Ann Womack

Thanks to Ryan, this has become the theme song of August "Young Adult Week" at Chalfonte House. He celebrated this song in his own life and in the lives of those with whom he journeyed:

"May you never take one single breath for granted ...Never settle for the path of least resistance. Livin' might mean takin' chances, but they're worth takin.'... Promise me that you'll give faith a fighting chance. And when you get the choice to sit it out or dance, I hope you dance."

4. *"Hands"* by Jewel

This song reflected how Ry put his faith into practice. It was #2 on Ry's first CDs and included on his **"Music for Heart, Mind And Soul"** mentioned above. Every line was a tenet of faith for him:

"We are all okay... worry is wasteful ... I won't be made useless. I will gather myself around my faith...we'll fight, not out of spite, for someone must stand up for what's right ...in the end, only kindness matters."

5. *"Me"* by Paula Cole

Ryan's mournful personal pain cries through the lyrics --- but *"Me"* ends in victory. Ryan was not a complainer, rarely sharing his true feelings. His poignant e-mail to his beloved brother, Chad, on February 6, 2002 a week prior to his major reconstructive surgery was an exception. This song reflects searing heartaches. ... but ends in soaring triumph:

185

"I am the silent one inside. And it's me who is my enemy, me who beats me up. And it's me who's too weak and its' me who's too shy to ask for the thing I love.

I am over the water and I'm scared as hell. But I know there's something better... you can't kill my spirit, it's soaring and it's strong. Like a mountain, I'll go on and on... but when my wings are folded, the brightly colored moth blends into the dirt into the ground. But I know there's something better."

6. *"Kind and Generous"* by Natalie Merchant

Ryan had written: "Not a day goes by when I don't thank God for all that I have."

First heard at Chalfonte as a single cassette release made for Jimeyer in June of 1998, Ry subsequently calligraphed the lyrics for him. This plaque graces the memorial wall in Jimeyer's Detroit apartment.

As one of the Chalfonteers confirmed: "This song expresses the kind of genuine gratitude that Ryan was known for expressing to those who provided us with so much fun and companionship in Elk Rapids."

"For your kindness, I'm in debt to you. ... for everything you've done, you know I'm bound, I'm bound to thank you for it...

Oh, I want to thank you for so many gifts you gave with love and tenderness... I want to thank you, show my gratitude, my love and my respect for you, I wanna thank you"...

7. **"Awesome God"** by Rich Mullins

This is the canticle of the church Youth Group in which Ryan participated first as member then as leader. Ryan was a mature and manly man with a capricious sense of humor. Permeating his life was a deep, submissive faith in God and in his church. His subservience to God was uncompromised as he sang in his heart:

"Our God is an Awesome God; He reigns from heaven above with wisdom, power and love."

8. *"There Is a Way"* by Tony Melendez

This guitarist and songwriter, who has performed for the Pope and around the world inspired Ryan. Tony Melendez has neither arms nor prostheses. Ry has a signed copy of his autobiography. Throughout the lifetime of his disease, Ryan marched to this drumbeat with head held high. The song proclaims:

"Too many times we don't finish the race. We just let the world determine where we place. Too many times, we believe the odds and accept defeat and never question the cause. There is a way to rise above defeat for all who dare to see -- for those who will believe."

9. *"Always Here With Me"* by Tony Melendez.

" Lord, I know you're here like a Shepherd leading me out of my fears into Your peace".

Ryan included this "Good Shepherd Psalm 23." in the CDs he burned for **"Heart, Mind and Soul…".** It was his ultimate hope and joy. The chorus proclaims:

187

"And when I walk through the valley where the shadows hang like death, I will trust that You're with me, my soul will know your rest...."

10. **"I'm Free"** by Jon Secada

Another of Ryan's hymns of ultimate victory. Ryan saw victory beyond his doubts and liberation beyond his fears.

"Do you see what I see? A rainbow shining over us in the middle of a hopeless storm."

Ryan's vision brings hope to all of us ---- for he saw beyond the limits of our sight.

"Do you need a friend right now? If you get lost, just call me; I'll be there. 'Cause I'm free I'm free! We'll have a breath of sunshine when the rain goes away. I pray I pray...."

11. **"Circle of Life"** by Elton John

"There's more to see than can ever be seen".

Ryan included this song on both **"Music for Heart, Mind And Soul"** and **"The Music for Chalfonte House."** I think I know the reason. The lyrics resound:

"It moves us all --- through despair and hope -- through faith and love ---till we find our place on the path unwinding --- in the circle of life."

12. **"Angel"** by Sarah McLachlan

From the day he died and continuing today, Ryan's family has been consoled through the documented "coincidences" of hearing this song at unexpected times and in unrelated places. It is as if Ryan's voice can be heard from the beyond: *"May this message I leave for you, dad, bring you comfort and consolation. Mom, may you hear it too"*:

"Oh beautiful release.... let me be empty and weightless and maybe I'll find some peace tonight in the arms of an angel," Ryan calls to them, who have vivid memories of his last weary days and sleepless nights.

And mom and dad whisper back to their beloved son: *"You're in the arms of the angel, may you find some comfort there."*

13. *"To Where You Are"* by Josh Groban

Ryan's gift in his last days on earth to those he held dear. He taught us this song in those painful days of August 22 - 24, 2002 between the time he died and the hour his death was declared. He taught it at his bedside in the Cardiac Care Unit of Beaumont Hospital, Troy, Michigan. Repeatedly coming through the small radio the hospital had placed by his bed, it was the only song to which we adverted as we maintained our vigil and commenced our separation.

"As my heart holds you, just one beat away, I cherish all you gave me everyday, 'cause you are mine, forever love, watching me from up above. Fly me up to where you are, beyond the distant star I wish upon tonight, to see you smile, if only for awhile, to know you're there, a breath away's not far, to where you are."

The afternoon of Ryan's funeral, August 28, (continued):

These past few days I have been neglecting my older sibling, Sr. Jean, who is critically ill in the infirmary at the Immaculate Heart of Mary Sisters' (IHM) motherhouse in Monroe, Michigan. I arrived at 4: 30 p.m.. What a contrast to the crowds supporting me at Ryan's! She is a dying woman, all alone in her eyes-blind and heart-compromised world.

"You have had a hard week," is all that she could muster. Then, "I'm very sick."   I sat in silence for half an hour with my hand on her arm as she lie there, nodding off to sleep. I kissed her forehead and she acknowledged my departure.

I shopped at Meijer's Department Store in Monroe, not because I needed anything, but in order to do something over which I had control. I never shop there. It was not on my way home. The banner over the entranceway announced: "*LEE ANN WOMACK (singer of "I Hope You Dance") TO BE HERE TOMORROW*."   I noted that and rejoiced that Ryan was at my side.

I had left the funeral luncheon exhausted and wanting to be alone. I was not interested in church music, Ry's music or any other noise. I paid scant attention to "***Being Held By An Angel***" coursing through my head. After visiting my sister, I arrived home, ate dinner and watched "***Back to the Future***" to force me to stay up until my customary 10 p.m. bedtime hour.

Since Ry's crisis, I have been experiencing night sweats. This night was the worst. Three times I needed to change my pajama tops and pillowcases because they were soaked.

I woke up every hour and a half. At 3 a.m., the diarrhea started. From 5 to 6 a.m., I slept soundly. I arose refreshed. In the intervening months I continue to have uncharacteristic energy and creativity, especially while authoring this book.

I Loved a Boy

Chapter 33: Journal of Grieving: More Coincidences & Sweet Sleep

Thursday, August 29:

When so much is out of control, one grasps at what one can. I cleaned the toilet and did the laundry. I told Rich on the phone it is as if Ryan's telling me: "Get on with your life. We've had a great ride, but it's over. You've got other people to deal with. You're officiating at a baptism tonight and a wedding in Traverse City on Saturday."

I am a thorough launderer. After sorting whites from colors, I empty all pockets, turning shirts and pants inside out. This morning, upon extracting the last wash load, a State of Virginia US quarter shines at me from the bottom of the tub. Thank you, Ryan.

This afternoon I prayed that if I could hold Ry alive in my arms, I would accept my own death here and now. I added a caveat. *"Lord, if you take me up on this offer, unlike Ryan, please make it happen without a lot of pain. I'm not into pain. Thank You, Lord. Amen."*

My distraction during prayer was looking through my patio window at a singular cloud formation. It had the contours of a dead Ryan last Saturday morning. His small head, his telltale curved shoulder, his arms, legs and tiny torso. And it appeared from nothing and got bigger and bigger until it exploded and evaporated into the ether. Thank you, Jesus! Thank you, Ryan.

192

Friday, August 30:

My first return to Chalfonte House since "it" happened. I enter the "geriatric living room" adjacent to my bedroom. I genuflect and kiss the corner of the couch where two weeks ago Ry knelt throughout the nights sucking at the air and trying to get some sleep.

Within weeks after his major surgery of February 12, Ryan's airway had become so compromised, he resigned himself to sleeping vertically. He knelt on the floor, positioning his head against the end of the couch for support. It tore my heart out to observe him there all night. I was consoled by his quip in an earlier email:" I've started sleeping vertical; I'm beginning to like it." I took his memo at face value. I shouldn't have.

As I walk down Elm Street to the beach, I hold my chest and gasp. It was the walk Ry often made alone. Gazing at Lake Michigan, I contemplate Erin's dream. A Ryan adorned with rainbow colors of the Chalfonte kids then enfolded in the darkness beneath the gentle waves. These waters are the same today as they were millennia ago, flowing to the shore and out again. Hart Crane's tribute to Herman Melville emerges from the seas of my thoughts.

"At Melville's Tomb"

Often beneath the wave, wide from this ledge
The dice of drowned men's bones he saw bequeath
An embassy. Their numbers as he watched,
Beat on the dusty shore and were obscured.

And wrecks passed without sound of bells,
The calyx of death's bounty giving back

I Loved a Boy

A scattered chapter, livid hieroglyph,
The portent wound in corridors of shells.

Then in the circuit calm of one vast coil,
Its lashings charmed and malice reconciled,
Frosted eyes there were that lifted altars;
And silent answers crept across the stars.
Compass, quadrant and sextant contrive
No farther tides . . . High in the azure steeps,
Monody shall not wake the mariner.
This fabulous shadow only the sea keeps.

Paul and Patti Hresko were the prefect people with whom
to spend the evening. They supported me through dinner
and well into the night. Laughter and copious tears on the
veranda. The breathtaking view of the harbor at sunset. It
was Laurel Pointe Inn in Victoria, B.C. revisited --- Ry and
me in June of 1998.

I returned to dark and empty Chalfonte House. Paul and
Patti walked me home. They chattered so late into the night
I could hardly see. Lying in bed, I forced my mind not to
dwell on the adjacent room where the tiny figure of my
beloved knelt throughout the night attempting to snatch
moments of rest by siphoning oxygen through occluded
nostrils and an unforgiving airway. God, we take so much
for granted.

Sleep, sleepless, sleep apnea, sleep disorders. Question:
How does a dyslexic agnostic insomniac spend his nights?
Answer: Tossing and turning trying to figure out if there
really is a Dog.

As a child during the Depression, I observed the anguish of
my mother's sleeplessness engendered by her worrying
whether dad would come home without a job. I vowed to

194

never be an insomniac. I have been able to keep that promise. Bed is exclusively for sleeping; well, at least for me.

In one of the foolish challenges of college days I tried to see how long one could stay up? I lasted forty-three hours. Toward the end, I was hallucinating. The slightest noise resounded in my head like fireworks. My mind was frayed. What simple and insidious torture it is to deprive another of sleep!

Ryan was hypersensitive to light. With recent Chalfonte renovations, I commissioned "Ray the Blind Man" to install the most effective room-darkening window treatments available in "the geriatric living room" where Ry often spent the night.

Narrating our adventures on the train ride, I described Ryan's snoring the time we shared the bed. I did not indicate when or how his snoring ended, then and every night. Because his oral anatomy was so compromised, Ryan was a "nose breather." By the wee hours he was severely congested. He would turn over on his belly, scrunch his knees and elbows along side his body like a puppy, and for the remainder of the night bury his face in a pillow to keep out the light.

I snapped a picture of him sleeping, modestly clad butt facing the camera. It is the final photo in my train trip album. The caption reads: "The End".

"The End"
Ryan attached to his nocturnal feeding pump

Chapter 34: Journal of Grieving: Dawn Breaks

Saturday, August 31:

It was my best night of sleep since this ugly episode began. The sweet freshness of the sun-filled morning; birds and the activity of rustling leaves and life. Conversations of John and Karen Burgess muffled from behind the bolted door of my private quarters. I am glad that they are near. There's a card slipped beneath my door from their daughter, Holly. Never before nor since have I received a note from her. No way could she have known of Erin's dream. The verse inside is from the Song of Solomon, 8:7: "*Many waters cannot quench love, neither can the floods drown it.*" The tears flow.

Emptiness returns when least expected. Two weeks previously, Paul surprised us with tee shirts to commemorate our gathering and the game of gangster. Kids signed each other's shirts. Now I don mine inscribed with Ry's final written words: "To Jimeyer, my mentor and friend. Thank you for EVERYTHING you have done. God has blessed me more than I deserve. Ryan, (the Scammer)".

On this beautiful Saturday morning his message heralds: "I am not gone from Chalfonte; why do you behave as if I'm not there? My spirit is filling every room. It's up to you, Jimeyer, and all my friends to '**Pay It Forward**'".[11]

I photograph the shoebox filled with playing cards he sorted earlier this month. I reflect on Ry bringing order out

---

[11] one of Ryan's favorite movies by Warner Brothers, starring Kevin Spacey, Helen Hunt and Haley Joel Osment

of chaos, his last conscious gift to us, the signature of God, Who did the same at the time of creation. A toast: "To you, Ryan, with love much greater than my heart can bear".

Monday, September 2, Labor Day:

For meditation on this peaceful early morn. I traveled streets I'd never walked before in my twenty-five years in Elk Rapids. Scarcely any "people activity." For a moment a bright red ball of sun struggled to assert itself from dark clouds before being overcome with chaos once again. As morning progressed, the sun rose, a fresh breeze picked up and a "normal day" began.

The lesson for today from my absent friend was this. "Even in a 'town' familiar to you, have confidence to move beyond the customary places we've been together. Take comfort that I have pushed through the blood-red chaos and am ever by your side." Ryan, I love and miss you. Please continue to be near to give me fortitude!

A silver VW bug like Josh Sheldon's drove past the park just as I returned home.

Tuesday, September 3:

Paul, Patti, and two priest friends, Val Gattari and Bob Fehribach, are my crutches as I travel, sad and vulnerable, to "Ryan Giannini Park" (RGP) for the first time since the glorious weeks of August. The park is a twelve acre woodlot ten miles north of Chalfonte House donated to the Chalfonte Foundation, renamed after Ryan's death. His last night up north was spent with friends at the bonfire in the woods.

As we emerged from the car, all of us remarked about the pungent smell of a burning campfire. It lasted a minute or two. How nice that someone was using the beautiful fire-ring, I thought. We discovered nothing around but the cold dead logs as we had left them seventeen days previously. I sat where Ryan sat. It is good ---he is good.

Back at the house, prior to departing, my priest friend wrote in the guest book:

> I can only say that as the Samaritan woman in the Gospel, I no longer depend on Jim's dissertations covering the mission and ministry of Chalfonte. I have seen and experienced it for myself -- the "Gospel" (Good news) of this place. I leave with cherished memories and feelings of much gratitude for the blessing I felt during this special time. ---*Val Gattari*

Thursday, September 5:

We are creatures of habit. When I prepare for bed, I empty my pants' pockets and place everything on the dresser --- keys, wallet, coins --- in anticipation of changing into fresh clothes in the morning. This morning, donning my pants I reached into my pocket --- and pulled out a quarter! Thank you, Ryan.

Monday, September 9:

I awaken in profound sadness. I commence the day by reading the accumulated mail. One card hits me hard and I sob for well over half an hour. "Why Oh God, have you allowed me the love of one so beautiful? I am not worthy of his love. Oh God! Oh Jesus! Oh Ryan --- I love you!"

Tuesday, September 10:

As I arise, I kiss his graduation picture on my dresser. I feel his spirit has moved on and there will be no more phenomena. The unwelcome message seems to be. "Now it is up to you to carry on what I stood for."

But once again, the quarters. I can understand the two on the lip of the duck display case at Chalfonte House though I don't know whence they came? The one I discover in the pocket of my shorts comes as a surprise. "Oh", I say to myself, "that's easy to explain. It was the change when I stopped for lunch yesterday." Then I remembered. I paid for lunch with a <u>credit card</u>!

Chapter 35: Journal of Grieving: My Personal 9/11

Wednesday, September 11:

Ryan is dead. We can no longer do things together. I don't like it, but it's over. I hear him say: "carry on without me."

I drove to the Post Office at 8 a.m. to buy some stamps. I thought my grieving was behind me. But everything reminded me of him as I took my morning walk around the New Center Area in Detroit. The Humane Society truck passing on the Boulevard. That's the place where Ryan got the dogs and cats he fostered. The Rehabilitation Center where four weeks before I was certain he would get relief from the tautness in his neck.

"America's Best" the banner blares from atop Henry Ford Hospital at West Grand Boulevard and Lodge Expressway. Damn the hospitals --- that could not perform the rudimentary act of pushing air into the lungs of my beloved. Damn the phantoms sneering at me beneath the masks of "uncertain world-renowned procedures" that in reality acerbate occlusion of his airway.

I walk on, oscillating between loneliness and desperation on the verge of uncontrolled tears. "M Accounting Services" in the window. My beloved Ryan aspired to become a CPA. The "Enterprise Car Rental" office brings thoughts of "Rent-A-Wreck" in Florida with Ryan and me together last spring.

Passing the Fisher Building I recall that it was on the second floor I purchased the "Detroit 300" jacket that enveloped my beloved on his birthday. A woman strolling with her toddlers had the single word, "London" emblazoned on her sweatshirt. We were to travel there this coming year by invitation of my friend, Jim Krupka. We planned to ride the trains throughout the British Isles; just the two of us.

And most of all, the railroad tracks. Ryan's beloved trains. I pass the Amtrak station where we departed on our great "Rocky Mountaineer" adventure on a beautiful May morning not unlike this one. Then it was joy, excitement and anticipation --- and now it is nothingness.

I hurt. I feel dirty. I need to come clean. "Car wash - Exterior only $3.00." I pay. It is enough for now.

Rich Giannini comes to the city to have lunch with me at the Harmonie Cafe. He promised the Giannini's would be by my side in my last illness, whenever that might be. Being in his family brings solace.

Late afternoon of September 11:

I have watched Debbie Ajini grow from a shy teen into a strong and competent married woman in her thirties. I value her wisdom and insights. We travel together ninety miles to Lansing to a Michigan Pulmonary Disease Community Inc. (MPDCI) board meeting. We talk of Debby Schuler, who was as a sister to her, a CFer like herself but one who died in a failed double lung transplant at age twenty-one. We talk of Ryan.

She asserted;
>No doubt the spirit of the loved one who dies knows what we, the living, are thinking. It is likely that in

previous lives, we had a love relationship and that is the underlying attraction in this relationship.

Our purpose in life is to accomplish particular tasks. You were meant to be mentor to Ryan. He has learned what he needed to learn in this life experience, and now his spirit is moving on. The uniqueness of these love relationships will last into eternity, no matter how many times our spirits might come around.

I need to ponder this, but am comforted. I have recognized the greatness of the spirits of several who were special to me. I feel humbled, inadequate and unworthy of their love, let alone, their presence. It warms my heart to recall a moment of candor when Ryan confessed: "Jimcyer, you have never treated me as 'different'; you have always treated me as 'unique.'" If only I were able to embrace him in my arms once again!

We've talked about his gambling and we've talked about his music. There is one more thing. He collected pop and beer tabs. "What a considerate child", one of my elderly friends said, "little Ryan is collecting tabs to buy a kidney dialysis machine for an indigent patient." NOT. His sole purpose in collecting them was to accumulate one million to be entered into the Guinness Book of World Records. He would arrange the tabs on the floor in piles of ten, enter the number in his ledger, string them on long loops of yarn and hang them on the back of his bedroom door.

At the time of his death, he had tabulated 26,610. The family has decided to continue working toward his goal. I never let a tab go astray, even if it means wrestling it from a homeless man on the city streets collecting cans for deposit money. I am as methodical as Ry, placing them in a container in my front closet, never in my bedroom.

Thursday, September 12, 11 a.m.:

Does his spirit remain with me in this place? Whence the
pop tab on the carpet next to my bed?

Friday, September 13:

I am alone and lonely walking in the midst of the crowd in
the Detroit Cultural Center busy preparing for the Festival
of the Arts which opens tonight. The sand sculpture is
incomplete; two empty arms of an angel. Thoughts of
"*Angel*" by Sarah McLachlan, his song #12.

When you are despondent, Jimeyer, why don't you take to
heart the advice you pass along to others? "If you
wouldn't have loved so much, it wouldn't hurt so badly.
Would you rather have loved less?" Or, I Corinthians 13:4:
"'*Love is PATIENT, love is kind.*' ' Patient', 'Patior'
means 'to suffer.' According to Paul, if it ain't got
suffering, it ain't real love." It helps to take my own
advice, as it does to recall one cliché I believe holds true:
"*Time Heals.*"

Chapter 36: Journal of Grieving: Passion

Saturday, September 14:

In early afternoon, I visit Jean, who is dying alone at the convent in Monroe. She has sisters and staff solicitous for her welfare, but lacks the loving ever-present persons that surrounded Ryan at his death.

Oil change on the way home: "Cranberries Concert" heralds the bumper sticker on the car next to me in the station. "The Cranberries" were one of Ryan's favorite groups. Though rarely heard today, he played their music incessantly in the years he first came to Chalfonte House. A cranberries recipe on the radio while I am sitting over the oil pit. Am I pushing these "coincidences" too far?

I was honored to preside at the wedding of LeAnn Muck and Jason Kilarski. They chose "passion" as a theme and this is what they wrote (edited):

> When one is driven to work on a task and the activity itself is the reward -- that is passion. When an artist spends three months on a sculpture that she has no intention of selling, the piece exposes her soul, representing thoughts and emotions that words cannot express ---that is passion. When the audience is vibrating alive and alert during a singing or dancing performance ---- that is passion. When two people look at each other and feel the love between them grow such that nothing could ever separate them, even death --- that is passion.
>
> Passion comes in all shapes, sizes and colors. It is the

205

smell of a freshly mown lawn that recalls one's childhood with such vividness that the eyes moisten. It can be the focus of one's current action or it is yet to be discovered. One's passions are woven into every fiber of one's soul and body. It is our life's mission to discover and nurture those passions that each of us possesses. It is the reason why we are human.

Each person expresses similar passions differently. The racecar driver who exalts in winning, experiences a similar emotion as the concert pianist during a standing ovation at Orchestra Hall. The two activities are not interchangeable, but the emotion that is expressed is identically exhilarating.

At its zenith, passion should be woven into one's dollar productive work so that the very act of producing an income becomes passionate. The doctor who strives for cutting edge medicine, or the painter who makes art for a living. The jeweler who creates beautiful artifacts, or the gardener who can feel each of his landscapes.

When someone is operating on the passionate channel of his or her existence, it is obvious to everyone they meet. When one functions at this depth of their passion, in work, in life, in love --- it is then that one functions as truly human --- as God has intended us.

Chapter 37: Journal of Grieving: Gift of Life

Monday, September 16:

This morning I "lost it", when I revisited Ry's songs and my reflections on "***Angel***" and "***To Where You Are***". "O God, Ryan, I love you. God, I love you! Help me to be strong! Help me to believe!" I lamented.

Today I visit my sister, Jean, only four years my senior. She is an old woman. "I want to die today," she gasps. She is alone. I love her -- but she now resides in the narrowness of her insulated shell.

I read the words from the letter Cindy was proud to share from "Gift of Life: Transplantation Society of Michigan."
> I am pleased to report that both of Ryan's kidneys were successfully transplanted...(it said in part) Ryan's liver was also recovered and was given to a woman who is the mother of two children, and who was a restaurant manager before becoming disabled....

My head says that this is right and I rejoice with Cindy. I am motivated to make certain Vickie Tutag Lehr, my Patient Advocate, understands that at my death any of my organs are up for grabs. My heart screams another message. <u>My beloved Ryan has been carved up like a Thanksgiving turkey and, with forks in hand, devoured by the eager diners!</u>

"...who was a restaurant manager before becoming disabled". Hmmmmmmmm, I wonder if she served Mexican? Recall Ryan's refrain when curious people would note that he was not eating: "I don't eat Mexican."

The Gift of Life lady promised to find out, but returned none of my phone calls. Not to be deterred, Cindy made independent inquiries and received the following letter several months after Ryan's death:

Dear Cindy, Rich and Family,

It's nice to have names to write to. My first letter was so difficult for me to write for a lot of reasons. I started to write at least five times and would start to cry and had to put everything away. This has been a very emotional and overwhelming experience for me.

Having your life extended puts your whole life in perspective and I think it has to happen to you to understand. As another recipient said: "You don't sweat the small stuff." What a gift!

I was told very little about Ryan and would like to know all you have to tell. As far as Mexican menu items, we ran lunch specials of tacos, taco salads and burritos, but nothing on the regular menu. I can only assume that it was something Ryan liked. If I gain a new passion for Mexican food, I'll know what's up since Ryan is living in me.

As for me, I am the mother of a son Alex and a daughter Deanne and blessed with seven grandchildren, the youngest not yet two. During my evaluation they asked me why I wanted a transplant and I said I wanted to see my grandchildren grow up. With Ryan's gift and the grace of God, I will see them grow....

"As far as Mexican items, we ran luncheon specials…If I

gain a new passion for Mexican food, I'll know what's up
since Ryan is living in me." -- Don't you love the humor
embedded in this "coincidence"?

Chapter 38: Journal of Grieving: Closure

Tuesday, September 17:

Why was she here? I hadn't seen her in two years since she moved to Alabama from the apartment next door. Delois Greenlee and her son, Tony with a new baby.

I invited her into my office while I double checked her email address on my computer. She picked up a can of "Ensure" returned from Chalfonte from my recent painful visit. We had kept extra dinner supplies there for Ryan, so he would have less to haul on his frequent stays.

"Tony and I love this", she exclaimed. I filled her bag with "Ensure + Fiber." She tarried for a moment -- and was gone. I've not seen her since. Ryan nourishes in ways we have yet to discover. A new baby --- new life.

The rest of the Ensure will go tomorrow to nourish Josh. Ry and his dinners will vanish from Chalfonte and my apartment forever. And the weather report asserted: "We have had no rain since August 24!" If they only knew.

It has been painful preparing a contract for Jill to pay off the remainder of Ryan's loan for the car that Paul Hresko and I helped obtain for him in August, 2001. "JILL GIANNINI... acknowledges her succession of interest in the estate of her late brother, Ryan...." rends my heart. I resent it that Jill touches Ryan's car --- which he had not been able to drive since his February surgery. Yet he made monthly payments. For anyone but he to own that car seems an unspeakable profanation of the sacred.

I am obsessed by Ryan. I am working on "Ryan Projects" that he be bigger in death than he was in life. A reading from Dan Kaplan's favorite book, "***The Power of One***" by Bryce Courtenay, gives me comfort. Though our roles are reversed and Peekay's mentor and friend, the elderly "Doc" died, the words resonate in my soul.

> I was home again just as the moon was rising over the valley. The pain, the deep dull pain under my heart, had lifted. Sadness remained, but I was now proud that Doc had achieved what he wanted to do. And we would always be bound together, he was very much a part of me. He had found a small, frightened and confused little boy and had given him confidence and music and learning and a love for Africa and taught him not to fear things. Now I didn't know where the boy began and Doc ended. I had been given all the gifts he had. Now that Doc was resting right, I knew we could never be separated from each other.[12]

Wednesday, September 18:

Early morning meditation dedicated to the trinity of Tim, Jon and Ryan and my kinship with them. Jesus said: "And when I am lifted up, (upon the cross) I shall draw all people to myself." (John 12:32). Vs 33 continues: "By these words Jesus indicated the kind of death he would die."

Ryan's picture's on the dresser where I can see him from my bed. A trinity this morning within an early hour. Tim and Jon among the living can understand. They knew him and were bound to him. All three are men. I am a man. I feel the bond among us at this waking hour.

---

[12] ***The Power of One***, pp. 441-2, Random House 1989

Ryan, rigid in death like the wood of the cross. Non-productive: no voice, no taste, no progeny --- nothing left of life and growth, and yet? "If I be lifted up, I will draw all to myself."

I hold the precious bond among us in my hands and heart. What is senseless in its creation, leads to magnificent resurrection in its outcome. In apparent death, he, we, draw all peoples higher. From flaccidity and frustration springs unimaginable birth.

Thursday, September 19:

Mary Ellen Gaffney-Liroff took me to lunch today. She is former Director of the Social Work Department at Hutzel Hospital and a dear friend. I treasure her counsel and reassurance.

> You provided Ryan what he was not getting outside of his family; certainly not in the same way that he needed it. You provided him with understanding and acceptance in a world that either didn't see him or blew him off. As Ryan struggled with intimacy in a normal adolescent sexual way, you provided him with unconditional love, acceptance and intimacy that transcended the genital --- even beyond the physical, so that he could experience the depth of what love could and ought to be.

Mary Ellen helped me realize that my paternal, nurturing and human instincts merged in my relationship with Ryan. I was working to overcome my father who rarely expressed affection or affirmed me. Perhaps he didn't know how.

I'm making progress in my grieving. Driving M-59 past Dequindre Road to Josh's, I stole a furtive glance at Beaumont Troy Hospital where Ryan died. Previously, I shielded my eyes while passing that intersection.

Rains came this evening, the first since doctors had declared that he was dead. They came at 8:00 p.m., the hour that mothers are to leave the hospital and children ordered to their rooms to be alone. He was fourteen. We were sitting on his bed bonding over summer storms. Now I watch as waters bring life to lifeless lawns. I am alone on the patio of my apartment looking down the boulevard to Children's Hospital. The rain dilutes my tears.

"Oh Ryan, I love you, Ryan, Ryan, Ryan, I love you", I moan. The thunder clapped, the lightning shown. And night came down again. "Oh God, Oh Ryan, teach me to believe." A solitary thunderous clap at 9:00 p.m. --- and it's over.

Chapter 39: Journal of Grieving: Death and Resurrection

Saturday, September 21, 2002 - 7:30 a.m.:

The call I was expecting from Monroe came at 9:00 a.m.. My sister, Jean, is dead. I say "thank you" and hang up the phone. I telephone my sister, Mary, who is crying softly. Jean and Mary were close.

To clear my head I walk for an hour in Lafayette Park. As I am leaving, a silver VW bug goes by. Josh, friends and I will play euchre tomorrow afternoon. Spirits of the living and the dead surround us.

Sunday, September 22:

"If there were no crucifixion, there could be no resurrection." A trite phrase used this morning by Marianne Williamson of Renaissance Unity Church as I watched her television show astride my "CardioFitPlus" health rider. It strikes my heart.

... and whence the pop tab entangled with my keys atop my dresser? I hadn't seen it previously.

I finish my homiletic tribute to my sister, Jean. I am pleased. Now to Sheldon's house for euchre with Emily and Piecey. Josh is tethered to his bed on BIPAP (an external ventilator or breathing machine). He is wait-listed for a double-lung transplant at the University of Wisconsin. When I arrive he scams me with a fake phone call from Madison (Wisconsin) alleging they have a pair of lungs for him. My heart leaps out my mouth. "Josh, paybacks are

214

hell", I remind him.

I hope that my friends don't know of Jean's death so as not in inconvenience them. Jean never cared much for kids.

Friday morning, September 27:

I don't want to lose his presence. I won't allow myself to see him happy in heaven, because that would be abortive of the hurt --- too soon, too soon.

Sunday, September 29:

Marianne Williamson has a timely message. Her topic was "Jesus."

> Regardless of whether one is Christian, you don't have to bear your burden alone. I, Jesus, have been there. I have gone through crucifixion (death). My message is one of life and resurrection -- and I will walk along with you from death to resurrected life.

Euchre with Josh was good ---with Emily, Chad, Dan Timlin & Piecey.

Visiting Giannini's house is a disheartening experience without Ryan to greet me at the door. We laugh about his ashes in a brown paper sack on Rich & Cindy's bedroom dresser. I do not want to see his remains. Cindy talks of excursions into Ry's bedroom in the morning hours when she is fresh. My mind says this rummaging through his stuff is inevitable. My heart says this violates a sanctuary.

Tuesday, October 1:

Particular things make me very, very sad. Buttons on my

computer for short cuts Ryan showed me. There is so much more I want to learn from him. Personal and Chalfonte Foundation bank statements. There is so much more I want to teach him.

Wednesday, October 2:

I watch my "***Harry Potter***" video. It is one of three movies to which Ryan took me. The others were "***Liar Liar***" and "***Patch Adams***." Near the end of "***Harry Potter***", Professor Dumbledore says to Harry: "It does not do to dwell on dreams -- and forget to live." I agree with the message but nonetheless begin to sob: "Oh Ryan, Ryan, I love you. Oh God, God, God, please protect him." I haven't sobbed for days --- it is for me.

Thursday, October 3:

The verse on the card from Todd Bills and Carla Vollmer is my morning solace: "But we can know that nothing that is loved is ever lost and no one who has ever touched a heart can really pass away...." Ellen Brenneman.

Chapter 40: Journal of Grieving: Counseling

Tuesday, October 8:

This evening, with Giannini's, I attended a grief counseling program given by Alan Wolfelt PhD and sponsored by Desmond's Funeral Home. His presentation confirmed the conduct of my plus thirty-year ministry. Some of my reflections:

- Mourning is predicated upon one's capacity to love.
- With the death of a loved one, there is a loss of self. Part of what is lost is a part of yourself. The deceased was a mirror to yourself who helped you know who you are.
  You need to make a space for your lost self.
- I will <u>not</u> be the same person after Ryan's death. One needs to <u>integrate</u>, rather than seek closure.
- The cliché *"Time heals all wounds"* only works if you are doing the mourning work.
- Tears are sacred.
- Two major areas where people get stuck in their grieving are anger and guilt. (This thwarts any other spiritual growth, I might add).
- Re: "mystical experiences." Honor these stories, even though we cannot understand them.
- <u>Re-member</u> the person who died: "Listen to the music of the past, so you can sing in the present, so you will be able to dance in the future."
- Develop a <u>new</u> self-identity (for me that is <u>author</u>)
- Grieving is <u>soul</u> work, not headwork.
- Re: prolonging your grief. You have to let a person who is dead ---be dead.

Thursday, October 10:

I was rooting around in my "suede" sports coat pockets. Truthfully, the jacket is 100% polyester, bought with pride from Value Village, a recycled clothing store. I had emptied the pockets several times before. This time a pop tab pops out. Thank you, Ryan!

Friday, October 18:

I am approaching Flint about 11:30 a.m. on the highway to Elk Rapids. I call my brother, Bob, a clinical psychologist. "How are you doing?" he asks. "Kind of downhearted", I reply, "but for the awful circumstances of two months ago, Ry would be sitting next to me." "Who's to say he isn't? I truly believe it," Bob shot back. His words console me.

For the first time I dared listen to the recording of Ryan's funeral "*Sharing Service*." Emcare's words moistened my eyes. I lost it with Erin's telling of the luminous Ryan of her dream. Mara's song finished me off. "Oh Ryan, Ryan, I love you", I lamented as I drove on through my tears. I sobbed long and hard, protesting my love for him.

Chapter 41: Journal of Grieving: Blood Money to the Rainbow

The Giannini family had designated the Chalfonte Foundation as recipient of the memorial checks to honor Ryan. They entrusted them to me. I loathed making the bank deposit. This was "blood money", the price of his death. I was Judas banking the thirty pieces of silver, the price for the betrayal of Jesus, "the sum at which the precious One was priced".[13]

Rich shared with me he felt the same way depositing Ryan's insurance check.

"Blood money."

Saturday, October 19:

There was to be a 9:00 a.m. meeting at Ryan Giannini Park (RGP) with Dennis Grammer and Matt Shepherd to plan its development. It was 9:30 after a rainstorm when I got my act together to drive the ten minutes from Chalfonte House. I arrived and no one was there.

Returning west on Barnes Rd to US 31, a rainbow appeared over the waters of Lake Michigan. Again, the iridescent Ryan of Erin's dream. Had I arrived on time or been engaged in a meeting, I would not have seen it.

The rainbow led me home to Chalfonte before disappearing into another cloudburst. I arrived at the door enveloped for a few moments in sunshine. Half-hour later, it is gray and overcast. Paul Hresko and Patti Leahey's' wedding was

---

[13] . Matt 27:9: ***The Jerusalem Bible***

that afternoon. Paul, along with Ryan, was one of three permanent directors of the Chalfonte Foundation. They were close friends. The timing of the bow was exquisite.

But there is more. It remained overcast until nightfall, except for half-dozen momentary glimpses of the sun. One of those glimpses of bright sunlight streamed through the windows of the church at the moment Paul and Patti stood before me to pronounce their marriage vows.

In planning their wedding a month before Ryan's unexpected death, Paul and Patti had chosen: "***Gather Us In***" as their entrance hymn. The text and music by Marty Haugen, (GIA Publications, Inc.) is a hymn used at many liturgies:

> Here in this place new light is streaming, now is the darkness vanished away. See in this space our fears and our dreamings, brought here to you in the light of this day. … Call to us now and we shall awaken, we shall arise at the sound of his name….

Further, the Giannini family chose this song as the processional at Ryan's funeral on August 28. Again, unrelatedly, "***Gather Us In***" was selected for the fiftieth high school reunion Mass I was asked to celebrate last Saturday, October 12, in Detroit.

Are these coincidences like the rainbow, the sunshine, the music, the quarters and the pop tabs? I defer to more fertile minds than mine for an explanation. It is enough to recall a saying I heard more than fifty years ago:

> "FOR THE BELIEVER, NO EXPLANATION IS NECESSARY.
> FOR THE NON-BELIEVER, NO EXPLANATION IS POSSIBLE."

Chapter 42: Conclusion & Contentment

Chad confided the following; first to his Aunt Cathy, then to his parents, and then to me.

> When our immediate family was in Canada in August and each night I saw how hard it was for Ryan to breathe, I prayed that if Ryan were not going to get better, God would take him.

The ancient admonition springs to mind. "*Be careful what you pray for --- or you just might get it.*"

I don't believe in a God who separates persons who love each other, even in answer to prayer. I believe in a God of "com-passion" ("suffering - with"), Who walks beside us in our grieving. I believe Chad's confessional experience is more profound than it appears. It speaks to the depth of a love-relationship that would be the envy of any two siblings. Rather than Ryan dying within forty-eight hours, as occurred, as if God answered Chad's prayer, I believe the inspiration for the prayer itself was from God --- working through Ryan.

In other words, Ryan was preparing his beloved brother for the inevitable. He inspired the prayer in order to prepare Chad for his death. It is as if Ryan's spirit whispered:

> Chad I know how much you love me, and I, you. I will soon leave this lifetime and you. Be inspired to lift your hands in prayer and ask that God embrace me. Your prayer addresses acceptance by you rather than transition by me. And the sign of my abiding presence in your life is that I will leave you on your birthday.

The accumulation of evidence convinces me that Ryan died in the "fullness of time" referred to in the first chapter of

Ephesians.
> God's favor is given to us with perfect wisdom and
> understanding. God has taken pleasure in revealing the
> mystery of the plan through Christ, to be carried out <u>in
> the fullness of time</u>, (emphasis added) namely to bring
> all things together in heaven and on earth…[14]

Ryan's life on earth, at least in this lifetime, was complete
in twenty years. Ryan could not, would not, should not,
have lived another year, another month, another hour,
another minute longer than he did.

This is not a rationalization. I could be comfortable
wallowing in anger, denial and recriminations. I refuse to
do so. The pain of his absence remains acute, but this is far
from a bad thing. It keeps him by my side and within my
heart. Ryan has impelled me to write this book. Being over
seventy years of age, it is unlikely I would be inclined to do
so if he had lived many more years.

Thinking of him in heaven does not console me. As the
processional song at his funeral service proclaimed: "Not in
some heaven, light years away…." I believe that his spirit
abounds on earth to inspire you and me. I believe he
communes with God daily --- and with us. That's why we
make our profession in the Apostles Creed: "I believe… in
the communion of saints."

A Sufi verse records: *"When the heart weeps for what it's
lost, the soul rejoices for what it's found."* Beyond my
grief, I have serenity in his life fulfilled --- and brought to
fruition. And that is what this book is all about. I am
content --- and very, very happy.

---

[14] ***The Inclusive New Testament,*** Eph.1: 8-10

The Gang – Christmas at Chalfonte
There is life after death!
Top: Sophia Franklin, Cindy Giannini, Nickolas Franklin
Middle: Nort Upson. Rich Giannini, Jimeyer, Maggie Upson
Front: Len Sheldon, Alan and Lori Franklin, Lynne Sheldon

Lynne and Len Sheldon, parents of Josh Sheldon, sign on the trunk of the Tree of Life in the Trophy Room at Chalfonte House

Epilogue

The following six inclusions should be instructive. The first entry is the complete version of Lynne Sheldon's reflections on her relationship with her son, Josh, in the last four months of his life. Cindy Giannini, Ryan's mother, wrote the five poems that follow. Given the relationship between Ryan and Josh, these mothers' words are a fitting finale to the book – told in their own mother-voices.

Lynne Sheldon's Reflections

The moment a new baby is placed in his mother's arms is the moment bonding begins. Any mother who has ever held a baby with special needs, like cystic fibrosis, knows without being told she is going to have an extraordinary voyage with this child. I choose to believe God knows what He is doing and has given this mother the will to take this journey with courage and love beyond my complete understanding.

This is a story that starts at the end; the last four months of a twenty-five year pilgrimage with my son, Josh. It was a typical night. Josh and I had a regular routine. Josh would start his vest therapy and meds. I would go upstairs, wash up for bed then come back down and help him finish his bedtime needs. We would end by watching the news and Jay Leno's monologue {'cause Josh liked him}. Then either I would read to him or we would talk 'til midnight. We then said goodnight. I'd go upstairs --- to toss and turn waiting for the phone to ring with that all-important call for the transplant.

This particular night would turn into a nightmare from which we couldn't escape; the beginning of the end though we didn't yet know it. I had been teasing Josh about some candy he'd been eating and I told him to hide it so I wouldn't eat it too. Before I went upstairs, I asked him for a piece. He smiled that beautiful smile I loved and said no he was saving me those extra pounds.

I had just donned my P.J.s, when I heard the monitor beep. If Josh needed me while I was upstairs he always talked through the intercom. I thought because he beeped he was going to tease me about the candy. I stepped into the hall. Len was watching TV in the family room. I heard the intercom beeping rapidly. I yelled to Len in alarm: "Something is wrong with Josh."

Len and I entered his bedroom in a matter of seconds. He was bleeding profusely. It projected like a fountain of ugly red blood, spewing out all over. We had experienced bleeding over the past couple of years but we knew this was different. Len used a wastebasket to catch the blood.

I gathered Josh in my arms and said, "Oh baby tell us what to do? Should we call 911?" He could barely answer "yes." Then with all his strength he said, "I love you both!" I told him, "Don't say that! You'll be fine; we'll get through this."

The situation was ironic. Josh never said, "I love you" to us. It was a family joke, probably since his early teen years. If he called home I would end the conversation with "I love you" and his answer was always, "me too." I teased him about it but it was enough for me. I knew I had his love from the first time I held him at birth.

I knew for him to tell us out loud he loved us, he thought he wasn't going to make it. Amidst all this, I was yelling for Len to call Dana Kissner, Josh's doctor. He was looking in

226

the wrong place for the phone number and I snapped at him. Josh said, "Please don't fight." We calmed down and waited for the assault of the EMS.

Five or six large young men invaded his bedroom. They might be good in some emergencies but knew nothing about CF or bleeding from the lungs. In our terror, we failed to mention Josh had hepatitis C which was inactive. They were pissed when Josh mentioned it later at the hospital. Could it have been he was a little busy at home thinking he was losing his life?

He couldn't get a ride to the hospital where his doctor was because EMS can only transport a patient to a local hospital! Len had been on the phone talking with Dr. Kissner. She wanted Josh brought immediately to Harper Hospital in the Detroit Medical Center. The bleeding was slowing down but Josh's heart rate was dangerously high.

In my firm mother's voice, I told the EMS to leave. I will protect my child. I told them we would take Josh to Harper. I was certain we could get him there. We had been making those emergency runs for years. More confusion. They were on the phone to their superior. It was a tough war.

In the end it was Josh who took control. His doctor had given him the nickname Dr. Sheldon because he called the shots and made the final decisions for his care. Josh said "Just take me to Beaumont Hospital." He needed to have control of a situation so impossibly out of control. It was decided he would be transported by private ambulance to Harper once he was stable.

When we got to Beaumont I was lectured by one of the EMS techs for not telling them about the hepatitis C. To say I was furious is putting it mildly. First of all, the Hep. C was

227

inactive and secondly, that was the last thing on my mind. I can understand their concern but I was watching my son go through a horrendous situation. They should have been better informed and a little kinder.

Speaking of "better informed," Josh was asked how long he'd had cystic fibrosis? This is one of the reasons why it is a waste of time going to a local hospital. It is more than annoying when you are in a crisis situation to have to take time to educate the person whom you hope can save you.

About 4 a.m. Friday, five hours after the crisis began, Josh was stable enough to move to Harper. He entered through emergency and though he had to go through the BS of case history, he was up to a room as quickly as possible. Finally they left us alone. We all slept a little; Len in a chair and me curled up at the foot of Josh's bed --- the mother lion protecting her cub.

We told Josh we would not leave until we felt he was okay. A stupid remark; he was never okay again. We woke up when the morning shift came in to take vitals. Len and I said we would go home to shower, change clothes then be back in a couple of hours. We could not foresee the next phase of the nightmare was about to begin.

When we returned in the afternoon Josh wasn't in his room. We were told he was having some kind of a scan. We waited. Several hours pass. We couldn't figure out where the hell he was. Finally Dr. Kissner came in and informed us he was in surgery. We felt awful. We would have gone down to let him know we were back.

She said we had been misinformed. She was not taking any chances. Josh needed the bleeding vessels sealed off. By the tone of her voice I knew it was a life or death situation.

I Loved a Boy

Josh had an embolism the previous October. He landed in ICU but got to go home the next day at his insistence. He was giving his best friend Mark a surprise going away party that night and had no intention of missing it.

This was a worse bleed and Josh was not as healthy. When they brought him back to the room, he was a mess. He was uncomfortable and in a lot of pain. It had been difficult remaining in the position the surgery required. His breathing was labored. I didn't understand why he hadn't been sent to ICU? I would learn later that Dana did not want him in ICU because they would have vented him (put him on a breathing machine) and she was sure he would not have survived.

Thank you God for big favors! We had a great nurse, that night. In the evening Jimeyer came; our angel in disguise as an ordinary person but with extraordinary perception. We were not very successful trying to keep Josh comfortable. We took turns soothing him to no avail. Even the respiratory therapist seemed troubled at Josh's distress. He suggested to the nurse he be sent to ICU.

Meanwhile Len, Jimeyer and I tried to calm him. Suddenly he popped forward saying he couldn't breathe. He was panicky. Dana instructed the respiratory therapist to use BI-pap to let the machine help him breathe and quiet him. He fought the Bi-pap saying he couldn't do it. It was a living nightmare; the beginning of the end for my boy.

At this moment I knew it was a privilege to be Josh's Mom. It was as though at his weakest moment I was given strength and power to help him regain control. I was overwhelmed in knowing why God with His guidance, chose me to handle a dying child. I needed to believe enough in Him and myself. Beyond motherly instinct, here

229

was divine intervention. It was to be a gift...the gift of almost four more months.

The room seemed too crowded with people and machines; too scary and filled with the unknown. My heart felt as if it were beating as rapidly as Josh's. My mind was searching for the tool to help my son whom I loved more than life itself. A calm came over me as I wrapped my arms around my baby, pressing my cheek against his. It was as if we became one. I needed to convey peacefulness. I needed to remove him from the chaos, pain and panic he was experiencing.

I spoke softly but firmly. I told him he needed to trust the Bi-pap to help him through this. He needed to let the machine do for him what he could no longer do for himself --- to breathe for him. I kept holding him, talking softly into his ear. Once the machine was effective and his heart rate was coming down, I whispered that I wanted to remove him mentally from the room. He needed to visualize someplace else. I described places he loved; the mountains of Colorado and the cottage where he spent his summers --- places far removed from his current situation.

I don't know if Len and I could have handled those stressful and critical hours without Jimeyer. He and Len kept trading sides, sometimes rubbing Josh's back and arms so he could feel the love and peace we wanted for him. Silently we prayed to God for strength to get through the nightmare.

After many hours as the Bi-pap was taking effect, Josh quieted down. All three of us had our hands on some part of his body. We were attempting to bring comfort and healing.

Suddenly Josh looked up at us very seriously and said: "Shouldn't someone be praying for me?" Leave it to Josh for some comic release. I smiled and said I was sure we had all been praying silently for hours but if he wanted I could pray out loud. Josh wasn't taking any chances. He turned to Jimeyer and said: "I think you better say a prayer." So with his gift from God he said the right words we needed.

This was the first of many prayers Jimeyer would say over the next four months. He was with us in those first critical hours and he was with us in the last hours Josh's body was alive on earth. God didn't answer all our prayers but He sent Jimeyer when the light seemed to go out of our lives.

I clung to him that night because I was afraid to let go. I was certain I'd not lose him --- but we came close. It wasn't his time. We had too many "I love you's" yet to say. This was to be the first night of a month in the hospital. Either Len or I were always with him. I thank God for that month. It brought us closer together. Josh commented that all this may have happened to bring us closer together. After that night we never let a day go by without saying out loud, "I love you."

Cindy and Rich Giannini, parents of Ryan Giannini,
sitting in "Ryan's place" at the bonfire circle
at Ryan Giannini Park (RGP)

Meditations of a Mom by Cindy Giannini

The first of the following five selections was written at
"Mothers' Weekend" at Chalfonte, May 4-7, 2001 before
Ryan died. All the mothers (of special needs children) were
asked to respond to the question:

***"What would your special child (ren) have to say to God if
s/he were before the throne of God in this vision?"[15]***

> John tells of this vision. 'I, John, saw before me a huge
> crowd which no one could count from every nation and
> race, people and tongue. They stood before the throne
> and the Lamb, dressed in long white robes and holding
> palm branches in their hands. Then one of the elders
> said to me: 'These are the ones who have survived the
> great period of trial: they have washed their robes and
> made them white in the blood of the Lamb.
>
> It was this that brought them before God's throne; The
> One to whom they minister day and night in the temple,
> the One who sits on the throne will give them shelter.
> Never again shall they know hunger or thirst, nor shall
> the sun or its heat beat down on them, for the Lamb on
> the throne will shepherd them, leading them to springs
> of life-giving water, and God will wipe every tear from
> their eyes.

Cindy wrote:
> Here I am Lord. Is it I Lord? I have heard you calling in
> the night. I will go Lord, if you lead me. I will hold
> your people in my heart. (words of a familiar hymn by

---

[15] The "vision" reference was from the ***Book of Revelation***, 7: 9, 14-
17

I Loved a Boy

the St. Louis Jesuits)

As proclaimed in the Book of Revelation from John, I <u>have</u> survived the great period of trial, even though I did struggle sometimes with the job <u>you</u> hired me for on this earth. I repeat, you hired me --- I did not volunteer the job of doing your dirty work --- of being your eyes, your ears, your heart, your suffering servant. I realize it is a job not just anyone could handle (with all the stress and such).

How do you do it being the president of your company – the whole Universe --- with the motto, "*love it or leave it*"? I tell you, I really didn't love it. Well, I take that back. There were times I did. But the leave it part; I tried a few times, but I was doing such a good job (in your eyes, I guess) that you wanted me to stay. I was an example to others and had the power to show them just how lucky they really are and how they should count their blessings.

When others saw me, some pitied me and were glad they weren't going through what I was. My job allowed them to appreciate the bones in their face, so they could eat Mexican. They could appreciate the projection of their voice, so others could hear them speak. They could appreciate their personal appearance, so others wouldn't stare at them. They could appreciate their physique, so they could play sports (even though I was Mr. Computer Wizard and Master of Backgammon and Euchre, when I won of course).

But you know what? I had many, many more blessings because I learned so much at an early age, in such a short time that others, unfortunately will never learn in a lifetime. My clients and my very special clients (my

234

family) didn't like my job at all. They struggled with learning to just let go and let God.

By releasing my control, you constantly reminded me of your love through my illness and those who have been a part of my care. I mean, if it weren't for great employees like me in your company, the health care workers and the insurance companies would be out of business and the unemployment rate would be over the charts.

Now finally, after all my hard, hard work (which was totally unfair at times) I get my retirement with an awesome benefit package I can cash in on. My bonus is that I'm on the top with the president himself! I moved up in the ranks in your company very quickly just like one of your past employees who worked for you many, many years ago (two thousand, actually). I'm looking forward to meeting him, your son, Jesus. Now we can hang out together. SWEET.

This second entry was written in the ICU while Ryan was on life support:

My Dearest Ryan,

We all told you that we wanted you to stay,
but you and Jesus had other plans on Chad's birthday.
You were always so stubborn,
and wanted things your way,
and now you shocked us all,
even though there were so many who prayed.

The most precious gift God sent on this earth,
besides His only Son, was you;
and during your short time here, boy ---,
did he have many things for you to do.

235

I Loved a Boy

You touched so many people from the time you were born,
and as I sit here by your bedside in critical care,
my heart is at peace, but torn.

You were my suffering servant, and my soldier boy;
you were dad's special Christmas joy.
Chad and Jill have a special bond with you
that only siblings can share,
even though in their hearts will remain a tear.
They can always remember, wherever they are,
you are there.

Your grandparents, aunts, uncles, and cousins
respected and held you in awe,
because in their eyes you were so strong
and without a flaw.
You have so, so many friends that were special to you;
you volunteered for them, burned CDs for them,
and played euchre and backgammon with them too.

The computer was your voice and
helped express who you really were;
and now you have decided it's time to take a detour.
I thank you so much for so many things
from the bottom of my heart
for choosing our family to be born into
and be an important part.

We are so sad that you decided at this time to leave,
but that's OK;
because the most important thing
we need to hold onto and remember,
is that through our faith,
we'll see you again in heaven someday.

I Loved a Boy

We believe in miracles,
and you were one over and over again
and for that I thank you, Ry, my love.
We all love you, sweetie.

I love you.

Mom

Filled with gratitude, Cindy had this published in her parish bulletin on Sunday, September 8, 2002:

To Our Church Family,

Ryan was not a human being on a spiritual journey, but a spiritual being on a human journey. He accomplished everything he was sent to do on this earth in his short time here, and more than others will accomplish in a lifetime. Maybe not in the physical sense that we as humans tend to think of during our existence, such as completing his accounting career or undergoing the rest of his reconstructive surgeries, but he was here long enough for everyone to see Jesus in him and hopefully help us to see Jesus in ourselves and one another.

Besides being the suffering servant, he didn't sweat the small stuff. The #1 reason we're all here is to love and be there for one another, and Ryan did that over and over again by touching many.

For those of you that have prayed for Ryan at anytime during his 13 ½ years of illness, please know that the Lord listened to your prayers and kept him on this earth much longer than he intended. We thank you deeply. Many thanks also for celebrating with us at the funeral home and sharing service, and for your cards and words of comfort…"

Over his signature, Cindy included the following poem from Ryan with the 2002 family Christmas cards they sent out.

> *When I was 7 years old, I saw the cross*
> *And said OK God, you're the boss!*
>
> *Life sure was an adventure of ups and downs,*
> *Tears, laughter, smiles and frowns.*
>
> *I put my trust in Him and dealt with come what may,*
> *And now spending Christmas with Him is here to stay.*
>
> *I did bid Jesus welcome when he came to call.*
> *You can't even begin to imagine that happiness*
> *I want to share with you all.*
>
> *I know your hearts have been heavy at times because you can't see me,*
> *But come on now, I'm always with you,*
> *so go chill and enjoy a cup of X-mas tea.*
>
> *It's really sweet being in heaven and I'm having such a blast.*
> *We younger generation spirits, with our way of thinking,*
> *Sometimes get into trouble with the older spirits of the past.*
>
> *Hanging out with the angels is awesome and I must admit*
> *I've taught them a thing or two.*
> *As one of my WWE wrestling heroes would say, 'It's True, It's True'*
> *There is no greater joy than to be with the light of the world on His birthday.*

I Loved a Boy

Now we can celebrate my 21st on Dec. 24th with Him,
in our own special way.

Many of my family and friends are all around me now.
When you come and join us, all you'll be able to say is
Wow!

So quit getting all teary eyed as you keep looking at me in
the past.
Smile, laugh, think of our good times and remember
I'm free at last!

Be good to each other, even when you don't want to, every
single day.
Even though I'm very busy,
I'll try to rearrange my schedule and help you in any way.

Looking forward to welcoming you at the glorious heavenly
gate.
A big party is being planned for you,
So when your invitation comes, make sure you're not late!

And lastly, Cindy dedicated to me her entry into the
Chalfonte House guest book after the family's stay at
Christmastime, 2002:

"CHALFONTE REFLECTIONS

You were his future
We were his past
All of us were his present
But then he left us so fast

Bittersweet memories Dec. 27th through the 31st
Not seeing or hearing him, those were the worst

239

I Loved a Boy

His special chair and meaningful plaque
Impacts his positive power on us
which we sometimes lack

We walk through the house and call his name
Then walk by one of his favorite places--the-beach—
and do the same

We don't understand why he was taken from us at this time
But believe he was spared from something worse to come,
and know he's just fine

He LOVED Chalfonte and it means so much to him,
as you well know
And our gratitude to everyone involved there
will forever flow

We THANK YOU SO MUCH for being his mentor and
friend
For introducing him to the kids
who can just be themselves
and not have to pretend

Ry's strength, smiles and deep faith
challenge us to do the same
And in our hearts he will always remain

Love~ Ryan's Mom